This book never bogs down and never distracts – it *acts*. If you aren't sure about an exercise, don't worry – there will be an alternative just a page away. It reminds me of how you get a cork out of a bottle when it's stuck – yes, keep pushing, but constantly from a different angle. These small, rapid steps can quickly add up. My suggestion: if you feel stuck with your anxiety issues, give this book a try.

Steven C. Hayes, originator and co-developer of Acceptance and Commitment Therapy and Foundation Professor of Psychology, University of Nevada, Reno

Another highly practical, simple-to-read, and easy-to-do workbook from Michael Sinclair and co. Step-by-step, you'll learn how to take the power and impact out of anxiety, and build the sort of life you really want. Highly recommended!

Russ Harris, author of international bestseller *The Happiness Trap*

If you struggle with anxiety, fear and worry, *The Little Anxiety Workbook* is an essential guide to a path of personal transformation. This workbook provides the steps for how to live life in a larger, wider and deeper sense, so that anxiety no longer defines you or your choices. This handy guide will help you understand how anxiety becomes a struggle, and how you can free yourself, by taking effective and practical actions in your daily life. These actions will be guided by your own breakthroughs and growth, through the exercises and perspectives offered. Filled with discoveries, warmth and compassion *The Little Anxiety Workbook* invites you to be transformed.

Eric Morris PhD, senior lecturer and psychology clinic director, La Trobe University, Melbourne Australia, fellow of the Association for Contextual Behavioral Science and co-author of *ACTivate Your Life: using acceptance and mindfulness to build a life that is rich, fulfilling and fun.*

It doesn't take a 400-page textbook to learn powerful skills to change our relationship to anxiety and live full and meaningful lives. *The Little Anxiety Workbook* achieves this in, well, a little workbook. Using salient examples and easy-to-complete exercises, readers learn how to take back their lives so anxiety is no longer in the driver's seat. Readers also learn that the cure for anxiety is coconuts (not really, but read the book to learn more!).

Jill Stoddard PhD, author of *Be Mighty* and *The Big Book of ACT Metaphors*

What a punchy and engaging book! With a wonderful balance of straightforward explanations, practical exercises and case examples, I expect this book to pack a powerful punch for those wishing to develop a better relationship with their anxiety.

Dr Nic Hooper, senior lecturer of Psychology at University of the West of England, and author of *The Unbreakable Student*, *The Research Journey of ACT* and *The Annual ACT Diary*

The Little Anxiety Workbook is the perfect companion for any person who wants to get unstuck from anxiety. In today's world, we're surrounded by unpredictability, uncertainty and so many unknowns that learning to manage, handle and relate to anxiety in an effective way is the skill of the century. This workbook offers top-notch, compassionate and caring skills based on Acceptance and Commitment Therapy that can be applied in our day-to-day lives. It's full of exercises and tips, and I cannot wait to introduce this book to all my clients, friends and colleagues!

Dr Z. Patricia E. Zurita Ona Psy.D., author of *Living beyond OCD using Acceptance and Commitment Therapy* and *The ACT Workbook for Teens with OCD*.

Anyone who struggles with anxiety has tried many things to control it. This clear, practical, science-based book offers a new possibility for many – a shift in perspective can free us from that struggle. By learning to pay attention differently, make room for discomfort, focus on what matters and treat ourselves with more kindness, we can start living life better straight away. This little book could make a big difference.

Dr Ray Owen, consultant clinical psychologist, author of *Facing the Storm* and *Living with the Enemy*

The authors masterfully blend elements of compassion-focused therapy and acceptance and commitment therapy into a comprehensive approach to living more adaptively with anxiety and steering life in a valued direction without letting anxiety derail moving towards what is truly important to you. If you feel like anxiety holds you captive from living the way you truly want to live, then this book can serve as an expert guide to helping you get unstuck.

Dr Eric Goodman, clinical psychologist and anxiety disorders and OCD specialist, lecturer in the Psychology and Child Development department at California Polytechnic State University, and author of *Your Anxiety Beast* and *You and Social Courage*.

The Little Anxiety Workbook is an ideal, easy-to-read companion if you are feeling completely overwhelmed and **stressed**-out by the daily events of your life. It is packed to the brim with so many practical exercises and relatable cases to help you bring a more compassionate and effective response to your anxiety. This book will highlight the small changes you can start making today to live a life that is far more enjoyable and meaningful than the life your anxiety has been dictating up until this point.

Aisling Leonard-Curtin C.Psychol. Ps.S.I., chartered psychologist, co-director Act Now Purposeful Living, Peer-Reviewed ACT Trainer and co-author of Number 1 Bestseller *The Power of Small*

I can't recommend this book enough. It is extraordinarily practical in its approach to the experience of anxiety. You'll find it full of useful strategies and tools to help you revolutionise your relationship with anxiety, break free of fear and live your life fully.

Joe Oliver, founder of Contextual Consulting and co-author of *Mindfulness and Acceptance Workbook for Self-Esteem*

The Little Anxiety Workbook provides a multitude of helpful tools and techniques that will be invaluable for helping people to cope with the physical and psychological impacts of anxiety. The beauty of this book is its clarity and simplicity. The reader is helped to understand the important functions that anxiety plays, how we can relate to anxiety differently and how we can live a life that is shaped more by what truly matters to us.

Dr Ross White, reader of Clinical Psychology, University of Liverpool and lead author of *Acceptance and Commitment Approaches for Athletes' Wellbeing* and *Performance: The Flexible Mind.*

The Little Anxiety Workbook

The Little Workbooks Series

The Little ACT Workbook

The Little Anxiety Workbook

The Little CBT Workbook

The Little Depression Workbook

The Little Mindfulness Workbook

The Little Self-Esteem Workbook

The Little Stress-Relief Workbook

The Little
Anxiety
Workbook

Reclaim your life with Acceptance
and Commitment Therapy

Dr Michael Sinclair,
Dr Elena Gil-Rodriguez and
Dr Michael Eisen

crimson

First published in Great Britain in 2021 by Crimson Coronet
An Imprint of Hodder & Stoughton
An Hachette UK company

1

A CIP catalogue record for this title is available from the British Library

Trade Paperback ISBN 978 1 78059277 0
eBook ISBN 978 1 78059278 7

Typeset in Whitney HTF by Hewer Text UK Ltd, Edinburgh
Printed and bound in Great Britain by Clays Ltd, Elcograf S.p.A.

Hodder & Stoughton policy is to use papers that are natural, renewable and recyclable
products and made from wood grown in sustainable forests. The logging and manufacturing
processes are expected to conform to the environmental regulations of the country of origin.

Hodder & Stoughton Ltd
Carmelite House
50 Victoria Embankment
London EC4Y 0DZ

www.hodder.co.uk

Contents

About the authors   xi
Acknowledgments   xiv

Introduction   1

Chapter 1: What is anxiety?   11
Chapter 2: Asleep at the wheel   31
Chapter 3: The best friend you ever had   59
Chapter 4: Being more than anxiety   89
Chapter 5: Being willing   112
Chapter 6: Treating yourself kindly   138
Chapter 7: Creating the life you want   161
Chapter 8: The beginning   196

Recommended reading   217
Further resources   221
References   223

About the authors

Dr Michael Sinclair CPsychol AFBPsS CSci is a Consultant
Counselling Psychologist, an Associate Fellow of the British
Psychological Society, a Chartered Scientist registered with the
Science Council, and a Senior Practitioner on the Register of
Psychologists Specialising in Psychotherapy. Following a career in
the NHS, he established City Psychology Group (CPG), a private
therapy practice in the City of London. He currently serves as the
Clinical Director of CPG, offering therapy to clients using
Acceptance and Commitment Therapy (ACT) and other mindfulness-based approaches, supervision to other psychologists, ACT
coaching to senior executives, workshops for corporate audiences
and the general public, and consultancy to corporate occupational
health departments. Michael has co-authored seven self-help
books including *Mindfulness for Busy People* (now in its second
edition), *The Little ACT Workbook* and *The Little Depression
Workbook*, and is regularly interviewed by the media on topics
relating to psychological wellbeing.

Dr Elena Gil-Rodriguez CPsychol AFBPsS is a Counselling Psychologist and an Associate Fellow of the British Psychological Society. Following a career in hospital pharmacy, Elena was inspired by her own therapeutic journey to train as a Counselling Psychologist. Since qualifying in 2009, she has worked in private practice and academia, lecturing on various Counselling and Clinical Psychology university training programmes and serving as a director of London IPA Training. She has trained extensively in Acceptance and Commitment Therapy (ACT) and she currently practises at City Psychology Group (CPG) in London, providing high quality, evidence-based ACT interventions to adult clients working in the corporate sector.

Dr Michael Eisen CPsychol DClinPsy MA (Cantab) is a Clinical Psychologist with experience in both private practice and the NHS. His private work at City Psychology Group (CPG) is primarily with busy professionals, helping them to overcome depression, anxiety and other common difficulties using mindfulness-based approaches such as Acceptance and Commitment Therapy (ACT). In the NHS, he has worked with clients of all ages, from a wide range of backgrounds, and with the full range of mental health issues, but has specialised in treating violent offenders with serious mental illness. He has a particular interest in mindfulness and meditation, having practised them since 2006, and has undertaken mindfulness teacher training with the Centre for Mindfulness Research and Practice. He has taught mindfulness to NHS staff groups and patients, to corporate groups at Google and other organisations, and to clients in private practice. He is a co-author of *The Little Depression Workbook*.

Acknowledgments

Thank you to our families, friends and colleagues for their support during the writing of this book, and in particular to Louise Gardner for the wonderful illustrations and Nicole Perkins for her invaluable input. Thank you to all of our clients over the years, for their courage and commitment, without which this book would not have been possible. And finally, thank you to all members of the Association for Contextual Behavioural Science (ACBS), for being a truly inspiring community.

Introduction

Welcome to *The Little Anxiety Workbook*. We are glad to have you with us. If you are reading this book, then perhaps your anxiety has reached a point where it, rather than you, seems to be in control of your life. If this is so, then be reassured that you are not alone. Everyone experiences anxiety, and it is a perfectly appropriate response to some situations. But it can all too easily run out of control and begin to take over. We use up valuable time and energy wrestling with our anxiety, and in trying to avoid it we might avoid situations that are important to us. Our efforts to feel better can start to pull us away from the life that we want to live.

Although we will each experience anxiety differently, you might relate to some of the following:

- You feel nervous, tense and unable to relax
- You have difficulty concentrating or thinking about anything other than your worries

- You worry that your anxiety will make you ill, or that you are going mad

- You avoid doing things because they make you anxious

- Your heart pounds, your stomach churns, you find it hard to breathe or you feel chest pain

- Your life feels narrow and lacking in meaning

- You feel as though anxiety is taking over your life

If any of that is familiar, then we are here to help. You may have already tried many ways to rid yourself of anxiety, with limited success. You may even have noticed that the more you struggle against it, the tighter the grip of your anxiety becomes. Or you may have come to identify with your anxiety, labelling yourself as 'just an anxious person', and given up hope of things getting better. But, as you will see in the upcoming chapters, we are here to tell you that there is an alternative. You are more than your anxiety, and it need not control you.

A different approach

The ideas and techniques that we offer here are drawn from the *third wave of cognitive and behavioural therapies*, a group of psychological treatments that take a radical approach to dealing with painful experiences such as anxiety.

Usually, when confronted with difficult thoughts, emotions and body sensations, we do whatever it takes to feel better. We try to make them go away or change them into something more pleasant. The third wave therapies ask us to do something different: to simply be aware of our thoughts, emotions and body sensations and let them be as they are, rather than struggling against them or letting them control us. This is often referred to as *mindfulness*, although we will not use that term very much in this book. Instead, we will refer to the various sklls that come together to make up mindfulness.

The radical approach of the third wave therapies is derived from the meeting of Western psychology and Eastern contemplative traditions since the 1970s. In that meeting, Western psychologists saw that the Eastern traditions contained profound insights into the human mind, and powerful methods (such as mindfulness) for relieving suffering. They set about integrating them into Western psychological therapies, and the third wave therapies were born.

In particular, we will draw upon Acceptance and Commitment Therapy, which is usually referred to by the single word 'ACT'. Developed in the USA by Steven Hayes, Kelly Wilson and Kirk Strosahl, ACT uses mindfulness and positive behaviour change to address the core processes that keep us stuck in life. As such, it can be used in any situation, not just with anxiety, and promotes positive wellbeing that goes beyond the relief of distress. It has been validated, to date, in more than 400 randomised controlled trials (the gold standard for research on psychological therapies), including many which directly tested its effectiveness for people struggling with anxiety.

True to ACT, this book will ask you to stop trying to get rid of your anxiety, and instead to develop skills that will let you deal with it more effectively, so that you can live a full and satisfying life. You will learn how to let your thoughts, emotions and body sensations be as they are, identify what truly matters to you in life, and move towards it, while treating yourself kindly. And if that sounds unap- pealing – after all, it is quite natural to want to get rid of your anxi- ety – then consider this: perhaps your efforts to get rid of your anxiety haven't worked so far; and perhaps it's time to try something new.

How to use this book

To help you free yourself from the grip of anxiety, we will:

- Introduce you to relevant psychological theories and principles;

- Illustrate these with examples from our own clinical work (all case examples are composites, to protect the anonymity of our clients);

- Ask you to do brief practical exercises as you read, to help you understand more deeply the ideas being discussed;

- Teach you exercises that you can do regularly, to help you build the skills that you need.

To help you get the most from the book, we ask you to take on board four key principles:

1. Practise

We will ask you to develop new *skills* to deal with your anxiety, and that will take practice. It is not enough to just read the book and pick up some new ideas. You have had a lifetime's worth of practice at doing things in your usual way, after all, and so it will take consistent effort to learn some new habits. And once you have finished the book, you will need to keep on practising, especially at times when you are feeling fine, so that when things get difficult, you will be ready.

Think of learning to play a musical instrument: you could not develop the skills that you need just by reading a book about them. You would need to practise, practise, practise, working on your technique, your scales, and on particular pieces. You would practise all of the skills that you need, individually, over and over again, slowly putting them together until you could play fluidly, without needing to think too much about it. And if you had a big performance coming up, at which you were going to play a difficult new piece, you wouldn't wait until you were up there on stage to try it for the first time; you would practise and practise until it was second nature. It's the same with the skills in this book: at first, they might seem unfamiliar and awkward, but if you keep on practising them, you can use them with the deftness and confidence of a skilled musician.

2. Workability

We have a natural tendency to evaluate things – to judge them as good or bad, right or wrong, or true or false. But throughout this book we will encourage you to look at things another way. We will ask you to instead focus on what is *helpful* – what moves you closer to the life that you want to live. This is a focus on *workability*.

In particular, this is a radical departure from the way that we usually view thoughts and ideas. Usually we want to know whether they are true or false. We might ask ourselves whether our worries are *really* accurate, whether we are *really* a pathetic person for having these worries, or whether the ideas in this book are *really* true. But how will you ever settle those questions? How will you ever know for sure? We could go back and forth forever trying to figure out the truth about things. A more helpful approach is to simply ask, '*Does engaging with this idea help? Is this taking me in a direction that I want to go?*' We ask you to look at everything you do, including your thinking, through the lens of workability.

3. Trust your experience

In deciding what is *workable,* we suggest that you try it and see. This applies in particular to the ideas and techniques in this book. That is the surest, most direct way to find out what will work for you, and it leaves no room for talking yourself out of trying something new! If you try our approach and don't find it helpful, then that is no problem. But if you wait until you are sure that it will work before you try it, you will never try it at all.

4. Be kind to yourself

When we have a job to do, many of us are in the habit of speaking to ourselves harshly, in an effort to motivate ourselves. We might tell ourselves to get on with it, and criticise ourselves if we fail to do it as quickly or as well as we had wanted to. In Chapter 6 we will explore why this is not a good idea, and suggest that a more effective way to get the job done is to take an attitude of gentle encouragement towards ourselves.

In the meantime, though, we suggest that you try to be kind to yourself while reading this book. You might find it hard to consistently practise the exercises that we suggest, or you might not think that they are working for you, or you might find it hard to read the book itself. If so, then try to encourage yourself with a gentle, supportive attitude, much as you would a friend who was struggling with a difficult task. Remember that you are doing this, ultimately, because you care about yourself and want to relieve your own suffering, and that treating yourself harshly will just make it worse.

Going further

This book contains some of the most powerful ideas and techniques in modern behavioural science, but it is not intended to be a complete remedy for your struggle with anxiety. It could certainly turn out to be, but it is also possible that you will want to seek further help.

There are a range of other self-help books on the subject, many of which will give you more detailed information on the therapies that we draw on here – see the *Recommended reading* section at the end of the book.

No book, however, can replace in-person therapy. A properly trained therapist can work with you in a way that is tailored to your particular circumstances and experiences, in the context of a supportive and trusting relationship. And while the techniques and ideas presented in this book have been validated with scientific research, this particular presentation of them has not. Most of that research has been conducted on face-to-face therapy, rather than on self-help books like this one, and this particular book has not been the subject of research.

And finally, people differ in what approach will work for them, and so while this book may be a great help to you, it is also possible that another approach would suit you better. If so, then we hope that you will not give up on your efforts to improve your relationship with anxiety and will instead keep looking for the approach that is most useful for you right now.

We hope that this book will be of some help, whether on its own, or by inspiring you to seek face-to-face therapy, or as a companion to therapy, or as a refresher if you have already had therapy. However you use it, we hope that it will assist you in breaking free from anxiety and moving towards the life that you want. We wish you well on this journey.

Michael, Elena and Michael

1

What is anxiety?

Anxiety disorders are some of the most common mental health complaints: thirty-four per cent of us will be diagnosed with an anxiety disorder at some point in our lives (Bandelow & Michaelis, 2015). But of course, anxiety itself is far more common – because *everyone* gets anxious. In this chapter, we will explore why we get anxious, and why it becomes a problem for some of us.

Anxiety 101

Anxiety is, essentially, fear, and it is our brain and body's way of keeping us safe: when something appears that could be bad for us – anything from a snarling dog to a global pandemic – fear kicks in, and motivates us to do something about it. In the case of immediate threats such as snarling dogs, we often react reflexively, without much time to think. But in the case of most of the threats that we face nowadays, such as pandemics, unemployment, or climate change, we have lots and lots of time to think, and that is just what we do. In an effort to deal with the threat, we focus our thoughts upon it, exploring all possible eventualities, especially the most disastrous. This thinking is *worry*, and it fuels the state of *anxiety*.

You may have noticed that anxiety is often a physical as well as a mental experience: you might feel a racing heart, physical tension, shortness of breath, and nausea or your stomach churning. All of this is called the *fight-or-flight response*, because it is what your body does to get itself ready to deal with threats – it gets ready to literally fight them or flee from them. Adrenaline floods your system. Blood pumps rapidly to your muscles, which tense, ready for action. Your digestive system switches off, freeing up energy for your muscles to use. Your breathing accelerates, bringing more oxygen into your blood. None of which, unfortunately, is terribly helpful when the threat you face is not a snarling animal, but rather the threat of catching a virus or losing your job.

The evolution of anxiety

The fight-or-flight response gives us a clue as to why we get anxious: because we *evolved* to be that way. For many millions of years, animals have needed to fight or run away from threats, and so they evolved the feeling of fear, to motivate them to run or fight, and the fight-or-flight response to help them do it. And our human ancestors were no different; their worry and fearfulness kept them safe. Imagine what would have happened to a cave-person who was always relaxed and never worried: they would have not lasted long in a harsh environment teeming with predators, natural hazards, and (most dangerous of all) other people. Their anxiety protected them, and so they survived to pass on their genes, including the ones for anxiety, to us.

The smoke detector

Not only did we evolve to get anxious, we evolved to get *overly* anxious. Think of anxiety as being like a smoke detector – it alerts you to serious danger, and so you *really* want it to go off when you need it. If it fails to go off when there is a fire, you may not survive. On the other hand, if it goes off when you *don't* need it, for instance when you burn the toast, then you suffer some inconvenience, but nothing terrible happens. And so smoke detectors are built to be very sensitive. They may sometimes go off when you don't need them to, but they are absolutely guaranteed to go off when you *do* need them to.

Anxiety is like that. If our ancestors got anxious when they didn't really need to, that was probably not a catastrophe. Whereas if they *failed* to get anxious when they needed to, for example when a lion was nearby, then they could end up dead. And so our anxiety has evolved to be like a smoke detector: very sensitive, and liable to go off when it's not needed, resulting in many false alarms. This is part of why anxiety, in our modern world, can feel like a problem, going off at the smallest trigger and getting in our way.

Mismatch

Not only is our anxiety like a smoke detector, but in our modern world it might be like one that has been fitted incorrectly (perhaps directly over the toaster) and that now goes off even more than it was designed to. This is because of the massive difference between modern environments and the ones that our ancestors lived in.

We no longer have to worry about wolves, bears or sabre-toothed tigers eating us, but instead, via the internet and the media, we are bombarded by information about all the countless things that are going wrong in the world or could go wrong. Our minds, designed as they are to scan for threats and then think hard about them in an effort to head them off, do just that. We worry and worry, about everything from crime to the economy to pandemic illness. Our complicated lives, too, provide plenty of smoke that can set off our sensitive smoke detectors: we have many relationships to maintain, many projects on the go, and many things, it seems, that could go wrong. And through the lens of the internet and media, it always looks as though our lives *are* going wrong. We look at advertising, celebrity gossip and social media, and compare ourselves endlessly to others, worrying always that we are not keeping up.

The trouble with thinking

It might seem that modern environments cause us problems because they give us too much to *think* about. But the problem is not so much with the modern world as with our minds. Our distinctively human ability to think is a great gift, but it can also tie us in knots, and this is very much true when it comes to anxiety.

The beauty of thinking is that it enables us to engage with things that aren't actually happening right now, and might never happen: the past; the future; anything that we can imagine. This has enabled us to create all of the technology, institutions and culture that make our lives so different from those of our caveperson ancestors. But it also causes us problems, because we react emotionally to our thoughts as though the events that they describe *were* happening right now. So if you think of a snarling dog, for example, you might experience all of the emotional and physical feelings of anxiety (both of which we will just call 'feelings' from now on), even though there is nothing there – apart from your own thoughts.

This causes trouble because it enables us to generate unlimited anxiety using only our minds. We worry about what is to come, imagine unlikely worst-case scenarios, and fret over past mistakes, all of which can keep us in a near-constant state of anxiety. And our anxiety, as we shall see, becomes a real problem not because it feels bad – painful feelings are an inevitable part of being human – but because it starts to interfere with our lives. We might spend much of our time worrying instead of engaging with what matters to us in life, and steer clear of the situations that we worry about. Unfortunately, these are often the very situations that matter to us, so that avoiding them leads our lives to become constricted and joyless. And that, we can say, is when anxiety becomes a problem.

How anxiety becomes a problem: disorder vs process

So far, we have talked about anxiety as a *thing* – a particular pattern of thought (worry), emotion (fear), and bodily responses (fight-or-flight) that can cause us trouble. And if you go to your doctor complaining of anxiety, they might diagnose you with an 'anxiety disorder' – a *thing* called, for example, Panic Disorder, or Health Anxiety, or Generalised Anxiety Disorder. Such diagnoses certainly have their uses. They tell the doctor what kind of treatment might be most useful, and they can provide comfort in giving a name to distress that otherwise might seem confusing and unmanageable.

But diagnoses also have their drawbacks. If we think that we have a 'disorder' called 'anxiety' then we might not think there is much we can do about it. We might see it as something external to us that is beyond our control. And if we should manage to rid ourselves of our 'disorder', then we are back to where we started: no longer 'ill', but no better than we were beforehand.

And so we offer here an alternative. We suggest that your trouble is not so much with a *thing* called anxiety, but rather with a set of *processes*: the habitual ways that you behave in response to your anxiety. And it's not just you! These processes are common to us all and very ancient: they evolved in us over millennia, because they helped our caveperson ancestors to survive and thrive. But some of the time, for some of us, perhaps especially in our fast-paced modern world, they can get out of hand. And that is when anxiety becomes a problem.

When anxiety is a matter of *processes* rather than *disorders*, we see that we are not 'ill' or broken, and that really there is nothing wrong with us; we just have some unhelpful *habits*. We see that while evolution, the modern world, and our own personal history might have led us to behave in ways that aren't ultimately helpful to us, it is in our hands to change things. And we discover that not only can we free ourselves from the worst effects of our struggle with anxiety, but we can go further. As we get better at responding skilfully to anxiety, we get better at responding to all of our other thoughts and feelings as well. We can go beyond the relief of a 'disorder' and take our life in the directions we truly want to go, and thrive in ways that we might not have thought possible.

But all of this might sound a little abstract. What, you might be wondering, are these mysterious *processes* or *habits* that keep you trapped in the grip of anxiety? Let's take a look.

1. Losing awareness

When we worry, we often get caught up in our thoughts and lose touch with the present moment, so that we have the experience of being physically here, but mentally somewhere else. We don't notice what is happening around us, what we are doing, and, most importantly, what consequences our actions have. Instead of engaging with our lives in the here-and-now, and doing what is necessary to take them in the directions that we want to, we lose ourselves in worry, regret and analysis and pay little attention to our actions. We act blindly, out of habit, and then find that our lives don't go in the directions that we would like. And from all this thinking we construct narratives about ourselves that we allow to define and limit us, keeping us from seeing and doing all that we are capable of. In Chapters 2 and 4, we will explore this process in more detail and show you how to counteract it: by connecting with the present moment, and seeing that you are much more than the story that your mind tells about you.

2. Getting hooked

As we have said, the problem with anxiety is not the thoughts or feelings themselves, but rather how we respond to them. And the problem is that we get hooked by them, meaning that we get overly caught up in them. We either buy into thoughts and do what they tell us, or we struggle with both thoughts and feelings, trying to change them, avoid them or make them go away. In fact, we often do both at the same time: we buy into our worried thoughts, which causes more anxious feelings, which we then try to get rid of with more thinking and by avoiding whatever we are worried about.

None of this is very *workable*. When we do what our worries tell us, we are likely to take actions that relieve our anxious feelings in the short term, but that pull us away from what we would really like to be doing. For example, we might spend our time planning and over-preparing, when we really wish that we could be more spontaneous. And when we struggle against our thoughts and feelings, our efforts are often ineffective – even if anxiety stops for a while, it always comes back before long. We cannot control our thoughts and feelings, or at least not for long, and in trying we waste our time and energy.

In Chapters 3 and 5, we will show you how to take a different approach to your thoughts and feelings: one in which you let them be as they are, as you do the things that matter to you.

3. Being harsh and critical with ourselves

As we said in the Introduction, we are often unkind to ourselves. And as we shall explain in Chapter 6, that can make it hard to do the things that would help us move beyond anxiety, towards a life that is richer, fuller and more satisfying. When we are harsh and self-critical, blaming ourselves for our anxiety and for our failure to fix it, we just create a new source of threat: our own minds. Upset and panicked by this attack on ourselves, triggering our own fight-or-flight response, we can't think clearly, we become less inclined to try new things, and we fall back on our usual, habitual ways of coping, which only serve to maintain our struggle with anxiety. When we are kind and gentle with ourselves, meanwhile, we feel safe, and are more likely to do what is less familiar: to make the moves that will free us from the trap of anxiety and create the life that we want for ourselves.

4. Not doing what matters

As you may be starting to realise, the problem with the processes discussed above is not how they make you feel, it is *what they stop you from doing*. They tie you up in efforts to control or eliminate your anxiety, using up time and energy and pulling you away from the things that you truly want to do. The more your life is about struggling with anxiety, the less it is about the things that you truly care about, and the more narrow and unsatisfying it becomes. In Chapter 7 we will focus on how to clarify what it is that you care about, and how to move towards it.

Don't worry if this all seems very unfamiliar, and like a strange way of looking at anxiety. It is a lot to take in, and there is no need for you to understand it all at this stage. All will become clear as we move through the book, exploring in detail these four processes and the skills that you need to counterbalance them. For now, let's look at an example of how they play out:

Nicole is at home, working on her report. She had planned to go to the gym and then meet her friends for lunch, but instead she has spent the whole weekend working, yet again (*Not doing what matters*). She had thought that the report was done, and was ready to send it to her boss, but then a colleague said something in passing that made her think that she might, just possibly, have misunderstood the whole thing. She told herself that it was probably fine, but she kept seeing, vividly, a mental image of her boss's face as he read it, and she imagined him thinking, 'Nicole really isn't up to this; we should never have hired her' (*Getting hooked*). That upset Nicole so much that she cancelled her plans and has spent all weekend going over and over the report, checking and re-checking and finding more and more to do (*Getting hooked; Not doing what matters*). And it is taking even longer than it should do because she keeps losing the thread and finding herself worrying about the report instead of actually working on it (*Losing awareness; Not doing what matters*).

She has a horrible feeling in her stomach, which she hates, and her throat is tight, and she keeps getting so frustrated with herself and her anxiety that she wants to scream (*Getting hooked; Being harsh and critical*). She keeps going to the fridge and eating unhealthy food in order to feel better for a few moments, even though she isn't hungry and has been trying to eat better (*Getting hooked; Not doing what matters*). One minute she is reading the report, and then the next she is over by the fridge, lost in worry about the report, her job, and her whole life, with a slice of cake in her hand (*Losing awareness; Getting hooked*). She keeps on angrily telling herself to relax and get on with her work, but the more she says it, the more upset she gets, because her anxiety just keeps on mounting (*Getting hooked; Being harsh and critical*). And the more she works on the report, the more hopelessly imperfect she thinks it is (*Getting hooked*). There is no way it will be ready on time (*Not doing what matters*).

In this example, Nicole is kept from doing what matters by her struggle with anxiety. She would like to see her friends, go to the gym, eat healthily and get her report done on time, but instead she finds herself caught up in anxiety about her report and in efforts to make the anxiety go away. She argues with her thoughts, she criticises herself, she overworks and she overeats, but none of these strategies work. Instead, they simply take her away from living the life that she wants to live.

Freedom from anxiety

Like Nicole, we would all like to be free from anxiety, and most of
our responses to it are efforts to make it go away. But often this
does not serve us well – we *struggle* with our anxious thoughts and
feelings, trying to get rid of them, and in doing so we engage in all
of the other processes that turn anxiety into a problem. And our
lives, over the long term, are the poorer for it. So, to prepare to try
something different, let's have a look at how you've been dealing
with your anxiety so far, and how it has been working out for you.

Work through the steps in the exercise below, and fill in a table as
in the example given – you can make one yourself. We have
included an example from Nicole, who we just met.

Exercise 1.1
Struggling to be free

■ Think of the aspects of your anxiety that you find most intolerable. These will probably include thoughts and feelings (by which, remember, we mean both emotions and body sensations). For example, you might have thoughts such as, 'It will all go wrong', 'If this goes wrong, I won't be able to cope', or, 'I am in danger'. You might have emotions such as fear, panic and shame. And you might have body sensations such as a pounding heart, dry mouth and knotted stomach.

■ Now think of how you try to avoid or get rid of these thoughts and feelings. This might include both internal actions, such as thinking reassuring thoughts, and actions that others could see you do, like going to the doctor for reassurance that you are healthy. It might include small things, like distracting yourself with the internet, or bigger ones, like not pursuing a career that would interest you because you fear that it might not work out.

■ What have been the consequences of these efforts to get rid of your anxiety, in both the short and the long term? Have they worked? Have they got rid of your anxiety for good? Have they cost you anything?

Thoughts and feelings that I find intolerable	What I do to get rid of these thoughts and feelings	What are the consequences in the short & long term?	
		Short term	Long term
Thoughts: It's going to go wrong'; I'm not good enough' **Emotions:** Fear; panic; shame **Sensations:** Pounding heart; tight throat; knotted stomach	Tell myself to pull myself together Work harder Distract myself by eating or going on the internet Cancel plans with friends so I can get more work done	Maybe my work is a little better, sometimes I feel productive and like I am getting things done I feel better while I eat and use the internet	I waste a lot of time and energy trying not to feel anxious Often my work is not finished in time and I fall behind I eat too much and I'm not looking after my health I miss out on seeing friends and doing other stuff that I enjoy as I work so much I don't enjoy my job

In doing this exercise, you might start to see how the four processes that can drive anxiety (as outlined above) play out in your life. And, perhaps more importantly, you might see that your efforts to get rid of your anxious thoughts and feelings might bring you relief in the short term, but do not work over the long term and have costs, which undermine your quality of life.

If this is so for you, then please don't be hard on yourself. Everyone gets into tangles of this sort with their thoughts and feelings, and everyone gets pulled away from living the life they want to live and being the person they want to be. Criticising ourselves for this will not help us change it. Rather, it will make us feel upset and under threat, and less able to explore the new ways of doing things that can help us to loosen the grip of anxiety. We are all in the same boat, and so singling yourself out for blame is neither necessary nor helpful.

The alternative: flexibility

There is no need to feel hopeless about your anxiety. Although your efforts to get rid of it may not have worked, and may have proved costly, in the coming chapters we will show you how to manage your anxiety more effectively, in order to do the things that matter to you. Will we show you how to:

F – ocus on what is right here, right now;
R – elease your struggle with thoughts and feelings;
E – ncourage yourself with a kindly attitude; and
E – ngage in the actions that matter to you.

All of which, you might notice, spells **FREE** – a handy way to remember the skills that can help to free you from anxiety's grip.

In a little more detail, this will mean learning how to:

- *Connect with the present moment*, so that you can see clearly what is happening and make wise choices about how to act, instead of automatically acting out your usual, unhelpful habits.

- *Unhook from your thoughts*, so that you can choose how to respond to them, rather than automatically struggling with them or being controlled by them.

- *Be more than the story* that you tell about yourself.

- *Be willing to have your feelings* and explore them with curiosity, rather than struggling against them.

- Treat yourself with gentleness and kindness – with *compassion* – instead of harshness.

- *Identify what matters most to you* in life.

- *Take committed action in line with what matters most* to you.

Taken together, these skills add up to *psychological flexibility*: the ability to respond in the most appropriate way to whatever situation you are in, so as to live in the way that you truly want to, instead of rigidly acting out the same old habits of anxiety.

And again: please don't worry if any of this seems strange or confusing at this point. We will be exploring all of these skills, and the processes that they address, in much more detail in the coming chapters.

So, all of that said, let's dive in . . .

2 Asleep at the wheel

If you suffer with anxiety, then you might spend little time in the present moment. Instead, your mind is likely to be focussed on the future, worrying about what might happen and making plans to deal with possible problems. Or you might find yourself caught up in memories, reviewing what went wrong in the past. And even when you are focussed on the here-and-now, you are probably focussed on your *thoughts* about it: whether things are going okay, and how they could be going better. In this chapter, we will show you how losing contact with the present moment can cause problems with anxiety, and we will introduce you to the antidote: *present-moment awareness* and *flexible attention*.

Thinking versus noticing

We often do not notice it, but our thoughts are continually taking us away from the present moment. You might have had the experience of driving somewhere, arriving, and realising that you have almost no memory of your journey. You were lost in thought, and unaware of what was happening in the present moment – we can call this state *autopilot*. And probably you had no control over it; You did not decide to slip into autopilot and lose track of what you were doing in the present moment. And whenever you snapped out of autopilot and noticed what you were doing, that too *just happened*, without your intending it. Your attention was hopping around of its own accord, attaching itself mostly to your own thoughts and occasionally to things in the present moment when they seemed more pressing.

We can contrast autopilot with *present-moment awareness*, which is supported by *flexible attention*. Present-moment awareness is simply *noticing* what is happening right here, right now, rather than *thinking* about what is happening, what has happened, or what might happen. It means using our five senses to make direct contact with the world around us and inside us. And flexible attention is what we need to sustain present-moment awareness. We need to notice where our attention is, and be able to direct it intentionally to where we want it: the here-and-now.

But perhaps this sounds a bit abstract – let's try it out.

Exercise 2.1
Noticing the breath

For this exercise, and for many others in the book, we will ask you to close your eyes or rest your gaze somewhere – which means, of course, that you won't be able to read the instructions for the exercise as you do it. So first read the instructions through, a couple of times if necessary, and then, when you are confident that you have understood them, you can close your eyes and follow them from memory. And if you forget what comes next at any point, you can of course open your eyes and check.

- Sit comfortably, or lie down if you prefer.

- Set a timer on your phone for five minutes (there are apps that you can use for this – see the *Further resources* section).

- Close your eyes or, if you prefer, leave them open but lower your gaze.

- First, think about breathing. You might think about how breathing works: the role of the lungs, the diaphragm, and so on. You might think about how breathing keeps you alive. You might think about how many breaths you take in a day. You might even evaluate breathing: is it useful? Is it pleasant?

■ Next, let go of thinking about the breath and instead tune in to the sensations of breathing, at either the chest or the abdomen. Notice the physical feeling of the breath coming and going. There is no need to control the breath in any way – just breathe your usual, natural breath.

■ See if you can stay focussed on the sensations of breathing for five minutes.

■ If you don't like focussing on the breath, you can do the exercise using the soles of the feet instead. First, think about the feet, and then tune into the sensations at their soles.

What happened? Perhaps, first of all, you noticed the difference between *thinking* about the breath and just *noticing* it by feeling its sensations. And then, almost certainly, you discovered how hard it is to remain in the present moment, just noticing the breath. And you will have noticed that it is usually your thoughts that pull you away. You would intend to notice the breath, just to *feel* it, here and now, in the present moment, but within a few seconds your mind would wander, and you would have forgotten what you were supposed to be doing. Your *attention* had been captured by your thoughts, and you had lost *awareness* of the here-and-now. After a while you would remember what you were supposed to be doing, notice that your attention had wandered away from the breath, and redirect it there. You would regain present-moment awareness and control over your attention.

This is what our minds are like all the time. We are lost in thought, and most of the time we don't even notice. When we do notice, perhaps because we had intended to pay attention to something other than our own thoughts, we might find ourselves powerless to do anything about it. We might pay attention on purpose for only a few fleeting moments, before our thoughts sweep us away again.

Habits of mind

Once you notice just how incessant and compelling the process of *thinking* is, you might become curious about what your mind is thinking *about* all day long, and how this relates to your anxiety.

Exercise 2.2
Where the mind goes

- Where did your mind go during Exercise 2.1 above?

- Perhaps you were thinking about the exercise itself: how easy or difficult you were finding it, how well you were doing at it, or whether it is a useful or a silly exercise. Or maybe your thoughts took you somewhere else entirely: into thoughts of what you plan to do later, or what has already happened in your day.

- Whatever thoughts you had, take a few moments to write them down.

- Are these thoughts typical for you? Do they reveal anything about your habits of mind?

- Did you choose to think these thoughts? Or did they just happen?

Most of the time, we do not consciously choose what to think about. Instead, thinking *just happens*, often without our noticing it, and our minds go where they want to. And where they want to go is primarily determined by habit, just like our driving when we slip into autopilot. We think the same kinds of thoughts over and over again, habitually, and each time we do, the habit of thinking those thoughts grows stronger. And so, when we are not paying attention, our thoughts go spinning down the same well-worn paths as they have always done, taking us with them.

The habit of problem-solving

If you suffer with anxiety, then you probably have a habit of anxious thinking. This kind of thinking is, above all, an attempt at *problem-solving*. We are trying to identify things that could go wrong for us, or might already be going wrong, and figure out what to do about them. And the problem that we are trying to solve, ultimately, is the problem of *pain*. If things go wrong for us, it is going to cause us pain, and so we try to figure out how to stop things going wrong for us, so as to avoid that pain. In fact, even *thinking* about things that could go wrong for us causes us pain, thus creating a problem for us to solve. And so any stray thought about a possible disaster is enough to trigger further anxious thinking, aimed at making the pain go away. It is our efforts to solve *imaginary* problems, ironically, that cause us a *real* problem.

Let's have a look at some typical anxious thought patterns, so that we can more easily notice them when they appear.

Worry

Anxious thinking is primarily focused on the future – fear is a response to something that *might* happen. When we worry, we look ahead to bad things that might happen, and then we might try to head them off by planning. You might find that you spend a good deal of time worrying and planning, trying to address all of the problems that (you think) might arise for you, but that your job never seems to be done. Your mind can always come up with more bad things that could happen, and more that you could do to prepare for them.

Regret

You might also spend time reviewing the past, in order to figure out what already went wrong, what might go wrong again in the future, and how you can be ready for it. After facing a social situation that made you anxious, for instance, you might engage in a detailed post-mortem, remembering every little detail of what you and others said. You might worry retrospectively, looking for all of the mistakes you made and the signs that things didn't go well, in the hope that if you can find them all, then you can do better next time. And yet, again, this process never seems to end: your mind can always come up with things that you have got wrong.

Judgement

You are likely to spend *some* time focussed on the present – thinking about what is happening right now. But this is distinct from present-moment awareness because you are thinking about what is happening rather than noticing it directly, with your five senses. And this too is part of the habit of anxiety, because all of our thinking (about past, present and future) tends to be *judgemental*. We are forever judging *this* to be good and *that* to be bad, and *this* to be better than *that*. And when some things are better than other things, there is always room for anxiety, because we want the best, but fear the worst.

Self-judgement

Our penchant for judgemental thinking, for problem-solving, is never more pronounced or anxiety-provoking than when it is directed at *ourselves*. Which, unfortunately, it often is, because we think about ourselves more than any other topic (more on this in Chapter 4). We analyse ourselves and our lives endlessly, judging ourselves for likeability, moral worth and various other qualities, trying to figure out where we fall short and have room for improvement. Here, again, we follow our caveperson ancestors. Their success and survival depended upon what their peers thought of them. The most well-liked and respected of them could expect to thrive and leave behind many children, while the most disliked and despised might find themselves cast out of the tribe, outside of which they would struggle to survive. Today, our survival might not be at stake, but still we are endlessly anxious about ourselves and our place in the world. And, even more unfortunately, much of our self-focussed thinking is harsh and self-critical. We harass and bully ourselves, hoping to motivate ourselves to do better, and while this might be useful at times, it often just makes us more anxious and less inclined to persist with the challenges of living the life that we want (more on this in Chapter 6).

In praise of the present moment

What, exactly, is the problem with all of this thinking, and why would things be better if we could stay in the present moment, 'just noticing'? How would we get anything done? Don't we *need* to think about the future, the past, and how things could be better than they are?

The answer is that we certainly need to think, but that our thinking is often uncontrolled and untethered from the reality of what is actually happening, right here and now. And this can lead us to act in ways that are not appropriate to the situation that we find ourselves in. We do not notice what is happening around us, we do not notice our own thoughts and feelings, we do not notice our reactions to all this, and we do not notice the consequences of our actions. Instead we operate out of habit, on autopilot: we think habitual thoughts and we act in habitual ways, often under their control. We react automatically, without awareness, and so we continue to act out the habits of anxiety, not seeing what we are doing.

With present-moment awareness and flexible attention, meanwhile, we see clearly what is happening around and within us, and we are free to choose how to respond. We notice our surroundings and the threats and opportunities that they present. We notice our own thoughts and feelings. We notice where our attention is focussed. And we can make a wise choice about what to do in response to all this, and then notice the consequences and learn from them. This might include *choosing* to think: we might decide to engage with a train of thought because it is likely to be useful to us. But we are freed from the tyranny of our thoughts. We no longer spend our time thinking (and acting) habitually, lacking the awareness to notice that it is happening, and the attentional control to stop it.

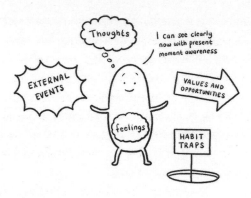

Let's have a look at how this works in practice:

Amir is sure that he looks foolish. He knew that he shouldn't have come out tonight, especially given how things went last week. He is just not on good form at the moment. And he shouldn't have worn these trousers. He wasn't sure about them, and now he doesn't feel right in them, and that's making him even more nervous, which, he knows from past experience, is liable to make him make a fool of himself. Everyone is going to see how awkward he is, or he's going to say something stupid, and then they will all think he is even more ridiculous than they do already. Maybe he should just leave. But that would be rude and then Clara, whose party it is, will really have had enough of him. He's already worried that she's annoyed that he didn't come to her birthday, and he didn't give a very good excuse because he was in such a panic that his text came out weird and abrupt, he is sure. He always does that, he thinks, and starts to worry about his text to Elton earlier this evening. Has Elton replied yet? He checks his phone again, and sees that he hasn't. This worries him even more.

Amir looks up quickly, and catches the eye of that girl he met at his cousin's wedding, but he doesn't say hello because he gets a mental image of himself at the wedding, making a fool of himself after he'd drunk too much. He feels a stab of panic and shame, and gulps at his drink. Maybe he should say hello, but it will just go wrong if he does, so he stays where he is and finishes the drink. But he looks up again, and oh no she's coming over. He starts frantically trying to prepare something to say, but all he can think about is not being able to think of anything, and about how this always happens, and how embarrassing it is. She smiles, saying that she always feels nervous at big parties like this, but he is already moving, blurting out that he has to get another drink, as he goes past her towards the bar.

In this example, Amir is thoroughly wrapped up in his thoughts, with barely any attention to spare for the party. And these thoughts are thoroughly habitual: worries and regret about his behaviour at past social events, negative judgements of his performance at this one, and worries about what is going to happen next. Barely noticing what is actually happening around him, he is controlled largely by these thoughts and his automatic, unnoticed reactions to them. When a young woman makes eye contact with him, capturing his attention momentarily, it is immediately recaptured by his thoughts, which trigger fear and shame. Habitually, he tries to dull these feelings by finishing his drink, not noticing what he is doing and why. And when this young woman tries to speak to him, he is so caught up in his own anxious thoughts that he doesn't even hear what she has to say, which is that she is nervous too. And so Amir misses out on precisely the thing that he really wants: social connection (why else, after all, is he so worried about what others think of him?).

How might things have been different if Amir had been able to stay connected to the present moment, and exercise some control over his attention? He might have noticed the anxious thoughts that his mind habitually produces at parties, and made a conscious choice to keep his attention on the here-and-now instead of getting caught up in them. He might have noticed his painful feelings of fear and shame, and the urges they inspire – to drink more, and to run away. He might have chosen not to obey these urges. He might have noticed that his anxiety was in fact a signal, alerting him to an opportunity to move towards something he cares about: the chance to connect with someone. And he might have heard what the young woman said to him, and been able to respond in a more workable way, perhaps by admitting that he also gets nervous at parties. He might, in all, have been able to notice his habitual anxious thoughts and feelings, and resist the urge to *act* out of habit, choosing instead to act in line with what really matters to him in the situation at hand.

We are all like Amir. Much of the time, we don't really notice what is going on around us or within us, and so we are yanked around by our habitual reactions, which can keep us caught in the trap of anxiety. But we can start to break free, by training ourselves in present-moment awareness and flexible attention.

Training attention and awareness

Fortunately, we are not doomed to remain forever unaware and inattentive, because present-moment awareness and flexible attention are skills that can be learned. But we will not develop these skills just by reading about them – we have to practise. It is like learning scales on a musical instrument: you will need to develop the habit of moving your fingers in a particular way, and the dexterity to do so deftly.

We have already introduced you to the basic method for doing this, in Exercise 2.1, above. We simply choose one or more things in the present moment to pay attention to – for example the sensations of breathing – and then do so as best we can. Again and again, the minds will wander and we will get lost in thought, and again and again we bring it back. In doing this, we learn how to:

- Pay attention to what we choose to, in the present moment . . . until the mind wanders

- Reconnect with the present moment, and discover that the mind has wandered

- Redirect attention to where we had intended it to be

You can practise this in a range of ways. You can put aside dedicated time for it, every day, or you can do it 'on the go', while you are doing other things. You can pay attention to sensations, sights, sounds, smells or tastes. And you can pay attention to just one of these things, or you can deliberately move your attention from one to another.

This is the basic component of *mindfulness*, and there are a number of excellent apps that are dedicated to teaching you how to do it, along with websites, books and courses that you can undertake in person or online (see our *Recommended reading* and *Further resources* sections for some suggestions). There are so many ways to practise mindfulness that we can't cover them all, but we can offer a few to get you started. Any of these, if practised regularly, is enough to develop all the present-moment awareness and flexible attention that you need.

Exercise 2.3
The body scan

As well as the breath, we can use the sensations of the whole body to train ourselves in present-moment awareness and flexible attention.

■ Get comfortable either sitting or lying. Lying down is a popular option.

- Bring your attention to some part of your body. You could start with the big toe on your left foot. Notice what you can feel there.

- Explore whatever sensations you notice. You might feel the touch of your sock against your toe . . . warmth or coolness . . . tingling . . . or nothing much at all. Just notice whatever is there, with a curious attitude.

- Now do the same for the other toes . . . the sole of your foot . . . the sides of the foot . . . and the top of the foot.

- Move through the whole body, bit by bit, exploring its sensations in this way. If you want to do the body scan quickly, you might scan larger areas all at once, for example, the whole of both feet at once.

- Whenever your mind wanders, just bring it gently back to noticing the sensations of the body. There is no need to criticise yourself – everyone's mind wanders.

In doing this exercise, we might become frustrated and self-critical, because we have been given a task to do, and we think that we should be able to do it perfectly. Notice how our tendency to *judge* everything, including ourselves, shows up here. There is no need at all, though, for self-criticism. Everyone's mind wanders, no one can remain in the present moment for long, and the point of the exercise is not to remain perfectly focussed throughout (because that is impossible), but rather to notice, again and again, that the mind has wandered, and to bring our attention back to where we want it to be. In fact, at the precise moment when you realise that your mind has wandered, you are already back in the present moment! So please be kind to yourself as you do this and all the other exercises that we will show you. The point is to *practise*, not to do things perfectly.

Exercise 2.4
Mindful walking

This exercise also involves paying attention to the sensations of the body, but it can be done on the move. Because it is done while walking, it asks us to focus on the feet, but you can include other sensations if you choose.

■ Start to walk, maybe a little slower than usual while you are getting used to doing the exercise.

- Notice the sensations of the soles of your feet as they make and lose contact with the floor.

- Keep paying attention to those sensations, as best you can.

- Whenever you notice that your attention has wandered away from the soles of the feet, simply return it there.

You can set aside dedicated time and space for this exercise – for example, you could walk back and forth across your living room – or you can do it when you are out and about. Any time that you are walking is a time that you can be practising. And, as mentioned above, you can experiment with paying attention to other sensations. For example, you could feel your breath while walking, or the motion of your hips.

Exercise 2.5

Exploring your mobile phone
(Adapted from Sinclair & Beadman, 2016)

In this exercise, we will tune into what is happening right here, right now, with all of our five senses. We will explore a single object – a mobile phone – with our five senses, but you can do this exercise using any other object.

■ First of all, notice how you are sitting.

■ Now take out your mobile phone.

■ Notice any urge to check your phone for messages.

■ Feel the weight of your phone in your hands. Feel the texture of it.

■ Now look at your phone closely. Really take in the shape of it, the light and shade on its surface, the colours.

■ Now see if it smells of anything.

- Hold it up to your ear and see if it makes a sound (you may have to rub its surface or tap it to get a sound out of it), or just acknowledge the silence coming from the phone.

- Put your phone down again and notice that you are now one phone lighter.

Try to do this exercise several times daily, wherever you are, and whatever you are doing. You can either focus on a single object or take in your surroundings more generally. The important thing is to step out of your train of thought for a few moments and notice what is going on in the here-and-now. To remind you to do this, you can tie it to particular activities. For example, you could take a few moments to check in with the present moment just before each meal, or when you get a message on your phone (before you read the message). Or you can use an app to set reminders frequently throughout the day (see *Further resources* for suggestions).

Exercise 2.6
Noticing daily activities

- Pick a routine activity that you do every day. For example, eating your lunch or washing the dishes.

- The next time you do this activity, pay attention, as best you can, to your direct sensory experience of it. Notice the sensations, sights, sounds, smells and tastes of it.

- For example, while eating, notice the colours and shapes of your meal, its smell, the taste and texture of it, and the physical sensations of chewing and swallowing.

- Whenever you notice that your mind has wandered, simply bring your attention back to noticing what you are doing.

This can be a great way to train your awareness and attention no matter what you are doing. You can try it out with more and more things, until almost every activity can become an occasion to practise.

Planning to practise

To build up your awareness of the present moment and the flex-ibility of your attention, you will need to practise every day. You might put aside some dedicated time for practise each day – somewhere between 10 and 45 minutes. Or you might practice several times per day, for a few seconds or a few minutes at a time, in between or even in the midst of other activities. Or, best of all, you might do both.

But, just as present-moment awareness and flexible attention won't happen by themselves, *practising* them won't happen by itself. If you just form a vague intention to use the techniques suggested here, as and when you remember, then you probably won't remember, and even if you do remember, you probably won't do it. Instead, you need a plan, and a clear sense of just why you are bothering to practise these techniques. You need to know what you are planning to do, when you are planning to do it, why you are planning to do it in the first place, and how you will deal with any obstacles that might get in your way.

Exercise 2.7
Planning to practise

Ask yourself, 'What is my motivation for practising these techniques?' The answer might be something like, 'To not be controlled by my anxiety', 'To improve my relationship/working life/social life,' or, 'To live a better life'. You can have as many reasons as you like, but they must be genuine, rather than the reasons that you think you ought to have or that you think someone else might have.

Write down your answers, and then complete a table like this one, which we have filled in as an example.

Mindfulness exercise	How many times per day	When?	Possible obstacles	How can I overcome obstacles?
Noticing the breath	Once	After breakfast	Urgent emails to answer	Keep phone on flight mode until afterwards
			Have to rush to work	Go to bed 15 minutes earlier
			The kids will be playing up	Ask the kids to occupy themselves for 10 minutes
Exploring the senses	Many times	Whenever I get a message on my phone	I'll forget	Write a message to myself on the home screen of my phone
		While I eat my lunch	I eat with colleagues at work	Just have the first two mouthfuls mindfully and then eat the rest on autopilot, talking to colleagues

Any questions?

Sometimes our clients have concerns about cultivating present-moment awareness and flexible attention. They worry that they will lose the ability to daydream, or to come up with new ideas by letting their minds wander, or even to think at all! Or they might worry, specifically, about losing their anxiety, which they think is a helpful motivator that keeps them sharp.

We should point out that these too are *worries* produced by your mind, and so might in fact be part of the problem that we are addressing here. Letting them dictate what you do might mean that you don't get to practise at all. But we can also agree that daydreaming, mind-wandering and even anxiety can all be very useful. It's all about how they fit into your life, and whether, in any given moment, they take you towards or away from the life that you want. And we can reassure you that there is nothing to be concerned about – you are not going to lose your ability to daydream or to worry, let alone to think at all. Rather, cultivating present-moment awareness and flexible attention will enable you to notice these activities of your mind, and make a conscious choice about whether to engage with them. If worrying, planning or any other kind of anxious thinking seems like a good idea at a particular time, you can choose to do it. But if it doesn't seem like a good idea, you will have a greater ability to notice it, and disengage.

Beyond autopilot

Much of the time, we are operating on autopilot. Lost in thought, we fail to notice what is actually happening, and instead navigate through the world acting out of habit. We even think habitually: when we are on autopilot, our minds run down the same well-worn paths, again and again. And, if you suffer with anxiety, then it is likely that you spend a good deal of time worrying about the future, regretting the past, and passing judgement on everything, including yourself. Lost in our anxious thoughts, we fail to notice what is happening within and around us, how we are reacting to it, and what consequences our actions have, and the result is that we may fail to respond appropriately. We act out of habit, controlled by our anxious thoughts and feelings, instead of making the wise choices that will take us towards living the life that we want to live, and being the person we want to be.

The solution is to cultivate present-moment awareness and flexible attention: the ability to notice what is right here, right now, and to pay attention to what we choose to, instead of being endlessly glued to our thoughts. By learning to pay attention on purpose, we can notice the situation that we are in, our thoughts and feelings, how we are reacting to them, and the consequences of our actions. And we can choose to act in the ways that we truly want to.

Takeaways
- Remember that we spend much of our time on autopilot – lost in thought and driven by habit.
- When we are controlled by our habits, we might fail to do what we truly want to.
- Instead of being controlled by habits, we can use present-moment awareness and flexible attention to remain in the here-and-now, and choose the most workable actions in any given situation.

3 The best friend you ever had

In the last chapter, we saw how our relationship with our thoughts can get us into trouble. We get lost in them, lose touch with the present moment, and act out of habit instead of how we truly want to. In this chapter, we will look in more detail at our thinking minds and how we relate to them, to see why it is that they have such power to pull us off track, away from the life we want. Which is to say, how we *get hooked* by them. And, of course, we will show you what you can do about it.

Your troubled friend

Just why do we get so tangled up with our thoughts? Why does it seem impossible to step away from them and connect with the here-and-now for more than a few moments at a time? Why are we so transfixed by our own minds, as though they were the font of all knowledge and understanding?

First, let's clarify just what we mean by 'mind'. We mean our *thinking* minds, rather than the part that of us that *just notices*, which we call present-moment awareness (as discussed in the last chapter). And the reason we pay so much attention to our (thinking) minds is that they *do* offer us a great deal of knowledge and understanding. If you want to make use of the information in this book, you will have to *think* about it. In order to write it, we had to *think* about it. In order to invent the printing press and the e-reader, someone had to *think* about it. How far could you as an individual, or the human species in general, have got without the ability to think? Not very far at all.

Your mind, we could say, is the best, most brilliant friend you ever had. A restless, irrepressible genius, bursting all day long with ideas and insights. And your mind has one desire above all others: to solve problems for you. All day long, your mind is with you, scouting for any problems that might be coming over the horizon and looking for solutions. When you are worrying, that is your mind trying to head off potential problems. When you are planning, that is your mind developing solutions. When you are remembering, your mind is scouring the past for clues about how to solve present and future problems. And when you are judging, your mind is deciding what is *bad* and what is *good* as a prelude to figuring out how to get from one to the other. And all of this is so useful and effective that we have come to listen very closely to our minds. All day long, our minds solve problems for us and we listen to them, just as we have been doing ever since the first proto-human looked at a sharpened stone and a length of wood and figured out how to make a spear.

Three cheers for the mind, you might say. But there is a catch, as you will know if you suffer with anxiety. Because our brilliant minds are kind of. . . out of control. Wildly creative, they are also deeply troubled. They throw up one idea or thought after another, all day long. Endlessly trying to solve problems, and find problems to solve, they go round in circles, they go off on tangents, and they dwell endlessly on what is wrong and what might go wrong. And we, waiting always for the next solution to the next problem, keep on listening, rapt. We find ourselves distracted from the present moment, gripped by worry, regret, and endless analysis, and unable to do the things that we want to. Listening to our brilliant but troubled minds, we allow our lives to pass us by. We think and think and think, and yet our problems persist.

Let's take a look at three aspects of our minds that make them both captivating and troublesome.

1. *Our minds can link anything to anything*

More than anything else, thinking is a process of making links between things. When our caveperson ancestor figured out how to make the first spear, they looked at a sharpened stone and a length of wood and were able to bring them together in their mind, before doing it in real life. And then someone looked at the object they had created and linked it to the sound 'spear'. And then someone else, a long time later, linked that sound to the pattern of ink (or pixels) that spell 'spear', and you, having learned the same linkages, see a spear in your mind when you read the word 'spear'.

And this is what your mind does when it is worrying: it might link the idea of *me* to the idea of *fatal illness*, or *financial disaster*, or *social embarrassment*. And those ideas themselves are made of various other linked ideas: a *fatal illness* consists of a number of symptoms, all linked together, with a cause (a virus, perhaps), an outcome (death), and a whole sequence of further linkages that specify *what you need to do to avert it*. Perhaps researching it on the internet would help. Or taking extra care with hygiene. Or checking your pulse regularly to make sure that something isn't wrong. We could go on, but you get the idea: this whole pattern of anxious behaviour depends upon the links that the mind makes.

The problem with this is that *there are no limits to the links that the mind can make*. It has the wondrous ability to link anything to anything, which means that we can *always* find something to worry about. You can see this for yourself with the following exercise:

Exercise 3.1
Invent a worry

- Here are four objects to think about: a watermelon, a platypus, a garden shed and the hobby of stamp collecting.

- Now, for each object, come up with a story about how it could harm you. We will do the first one, as an example: a crate of watermelons could have a dangerous tropical spider in it. Or the watermelon itself could be infected with dangerous bacteria. Or if you ate too many watermelons, you might feel full, but actually they are mostly water, and so you would not be getting much nourishment, and so you might suffer dangerous nutritional deficiencies...

Sorry, we started getting carried away there. But you see how easy it is. Have a go at the others before you read on.

And it gets worse, because not only can your mind always generate new fears about any object or idea, but, because it loves to link one thing to another, your fears can spread from one thing to another. This situation is *like* that one, and so you had better be careful, even though it is new to you and has yet to prove itself dangerous. If a crate of watermelons could contain a poisonous spider, then what about other fruit? Perhaps grapefruit are best avoided, and bananas too. Again, this is very helpful much of the time: having been chased by one lion, our cave-dwelling ancestor would be well advised to fear *all* lions, and indeed *all* animals with claws and big teeth. But it can become constricting: you did badly in an important exam, and now you fear *all* exams, and also job interviews, and as a result you avoid them, and so you fail to develop your career.

2. *Thoughts seem real*

As remarkable as our thinking abilities are, they would have little impact if our thoughts didn't *feel* like anything. When our caveperson ancestor made their first spear, why did they bother? Because they had thoughts like, 'This will improve my hunting, and so I will have more food', and the thought of 'more food' *felt* appealing, just like real food, and so motivated them to make the spear. And when they were warned by a friend, 'Don't hunt in that direction – there is a lion', those words called forth in their mind the thought of a lion, and they felt fear, just as if they could actually see the lion, and it motivated them to stay away. Much easier and less dangerous than having to see the animal in the flesh before the fear kicked in.

But once again, this wondrous feature of our minds leads us into trouble. Because if we can come up with an endless stream of worrying thoughts, and our thoughts carry an emotional charge, then we can generate a pretty much endless supply of fear – as you will know if you suffer with anxiety. Each time your mind comes up with an alarming scenario, you will feel the same fear as if it were actually happening. Let's experience this for ourselves:

Exercise 3.2
Scared of shadows

- Sit comfortably, and either close your eyes or lower your gaze.

- Tune into the sensations of breathing, and attend to them for a minute or two, as best you can.

- Now think of something a bit anxiety-provoking. Probably not the most alarming thing that you can think of, but something that makes you feel somewhat anxious.

- Notice what happens in your body and mind. Notice any thoughts, emotions and body sensations that show up. Most importantly, notice any urge that you feel to *do* anything.

In doing this exercise, you will probably have noticed your emotional reaction to your thoughts. You might also have noticed a physical reaction, such as your heart rate speeding up, your breathing getting rapid and shallow, and your muscles tensing. This is the fight-or-flight response, firing up just as though you were faced with a real threat. But there's nothing there – apart from your thoughts. And, most importantly, you might have noticed your urge to take *action* in response to your fear. This is the heart of the problem: when we feel fear, we are motivated to try to get away from it, and in doing so we often cut ourselves off from the things that we want to do, and fail to move in the directions that we value in life.

3. *There is no 'delete' button*

Because our thoughts multiply and spread, and because they can make us feel bad, we might understandably hope to control them. You may wish that you could stop your worries and replace them with more positive thoughts. Unfortunately, this is just not how the mind works. There is no delete button, and once your mind has linked one thing to another, you cannot break that link – when you think of one thing, you are liable to think of whatever it has previously become linked to. In fact, if you try to control your thoughts, then those efforts themselves just become linked to the thoughts that you are trying to get rid of, and become triggers for them. So if you are used to telling yourself, 'Nothing to worry about', in response to anxious thoughts, then the thought, 'Nothing to worry about' is likely to become a trigger for anxious thoughts! Efforts to control your mind will never succeed for long, and they eat up time, attention and energy that could be better used for building the life that you want. Let's see this for ourselves:

Exercise 3.3
Thinking and linking

We have a secret to tell you, and it's a big one. It's this: that the cure for anxiety is... coconuts. Yes, that's right, coconuts. Anxiety, coconuts. Coconuts, anxiety. Anxiety, anxiety, anxiety. Coconuts, coconuts, coconuts.

Okay, so that isn't actually the cure for anxiety. But what happens now if we say...

The cure for anxiety is...

Did you, by any chance, think of coconuts? Can you stop yourself thinking of them? Let's try it. Read the following, and try your very best NOT to think of coconuts.

The cure for anxiety is...

Probably, you cannot now stop yourself from finishing that sentence with 'coconuts'. Because this is how the mind works: it links one thing to another, all day long, and we have no way to delete the links. You could try telling yourself that 'the cure for anxiety is *not* coconuts', but that's just another link between 'the cure for anxiety' and 'coconuts'. Thinking of one will still make you think of the other.

How worthwhile, then, would it be to try to stop yourself from thinking 'coconuts'? And how easy or difficult would it be for you to get on with other things while you were doing it? What effect would it have on your life if you made it your number one priority to not have the thought 'coconuts' when you think of 'the cure for anxiety'? Now consider what effect it has when you struggle with your anxious thoughts, trying to change them or make them go away. You cannot delete the links that pull you into anxiety; you can only add more.

Let's see how these aspects of our thoughts play out in real life, and the impact they have on our lives:

Carla is thinking about her thoughts. She is worried that these aren't normal thoughts to have, and that they must mean there is something wrong with her. Would she worry so much about being seriously ill if she weren't, in fact, seriously ill? She is not sure just what is wrong with her, but she can't shake these thoughts that *something* is. It could be cancer, it could be her immune system, it could be that she's got one of those heart problems that no one knows about until it suddenly strikes. That would be awful. She imagines herself playing with her son and suddenly clutching her chest, stricken, his happy little face turning to confusion, then fear, then horror as she pitches forwards onto the floor. The thought is unbearable; she can feel her stomach twisting. She feels like she should stay away from her son, so that he is not around when it finally happens. 'You're fine, Carla,' she tells herself. 'You're fine!' But she knows she doesn't believe it. And why doesn't she believe it? Because it isn't true! If it were true, it would *feel* true. Instead she feels that she's lying to herself when she says it, and that she knows, deep down, what's really true: that something is terribly wrong with her. She has to do something, she thinks. She'll call the doctor. But they'll just laugh at her. She imagines what they must think of her when she shows up, time and again, at the surgery, with worries that don't amount to anything. Maybe they're right

– maybe she's losing her mind. Is this how insanity starts? Are her worries getting worse? She tries to remember when she first started worrying like this. It's been going on for as long as she can remember, but the first thing she remembers worrying about is her father and his heart, and he did die of a heart attack, in the end! So maybe it's not insanity – she was right then, and she's probably right now! She worried about him, and he died, and now she's worried about herself. She does need to do something about it, she thinks, and picks up her phone to make an appointment with the doctor.

In this example, Carla is thoroughly hooked by her thoughts, which are attempting to solve a problem. Her mind, ever the good and faithful friend, is trying to root out and address any dangers to her health. But, though her mind is only trying to help her, its efforts are fruitless and counter-productive, because it can generate endless stories about possible dangers, and because she cannot control it. Maybe the problem is with her heart, or her immune system, or maybe she has cancer. Maybe her thoughts themselves are evidence that something is wrong, or maybe her thoughts themselves are a symptom of mental illness.

Carla's mind could carry on like this indefinitely, and her efforts to argue with it go nowhere: when she tells herself that she is fine, her mind just returns to its anxious theme and argues back. And all of this packs the emotional punch of real danger. When she imagines suffering a heart attack in front of her son, the thought feels unbearable, even though nothing bad has actually happened to her, or is likely to. She even feels the urge to avoid her son, which is surely not in line with her deepest wishes for herself and her life. And ultimately, unable to bear her feelings, she takes action to make them go away: she phones the doctor's surgery. Even though her repeated trips there are doing little to enrich her life.

We all get pulled off-track by our minds, much as Carla does, but it does not have to be this way. Because no matter what our minds tell us, *we do not have to let them control us*. We cannot stop them from spinning endless stories, linking one thing to another and another, but we can choose how we respond to them. Even as they spin their stories, we can choose how much attention to give them, whether we buy into what they tell us, and what we actually *do* in the next moment, and the next. We can *unhook* from thoughts by:

- Stepping back from them.

- Deciding whether it is helpful to listen to them, in light of what matters most to us.

- Taking action in line with what matters most, even if our minds are telling us not to.

Before we start to practise unhooking from thoughts, it is import-ant to note that none of these techniques are intended to *stop* or *get rid of* thoughts. Rather, we are aiming to notice them, step back from them, and acquire the freedom to do what we choose to, even in their presence, rather than struggling with them or doing what they tell us to. So, when you use any of these techniques, you can fully expect your thoughts to keep on coming. But if you can learn to relate to them in this new way, then they need not cause you a problem.

And, as we recommend for all of the exercises in this book, you will need to practise these techniques often – several times each day – so that they become increasingly easy, effective and habitual. You can practise on any thoughts, not just anxious ones – the aim here is to see that *all* thoughts (not just anxious ones) are *just thoughts*, rather than facts or commandments. And then, when anxious thoughts threaten to take control, you will have the skills to respond effectively. We suggest that you make a plan for practising them, perhaps using a table like the one that you completed in Chapter 2 when you were planning to practise the exercises in that chapter.

Now, let's begin learning to unhook from thoughts.

Stepping back

Stepping back from thoughts means, above all, simply *noticing* them, using present-moment awareness. When we do that, it is as though we create space between ourselves and our thoughts, and in that space we can decide whether or not it is helpful, in this particular situation, to keep on engaging with them.

In the last chapter, we explored how we can either be lost in thought or connected to the present moment via our five senses. Well, in fact we can turn our ability to see and hear *inwards*, and 'see' and 'hear' our thoughts. Instead of being lost in thought, we can simply *notice* thoughts, as just another thing happening in the field of our awareness.

Let's try this out:

Exercise 3.4
Turning inwards

- Take a look around you. Take in the space and objects that you can see.

- Notice the colours that you can see, and the shapes, and the patterns of light and shade.

■ Now notice what you can hear. Notice the tone, and pitch, and volume of the sounds that you hear around you.

■ Notice anything that you can smell.

■ Can you taste anything?

■ Next, tune into the sensations of your body. Notice the sensations of your body making contact with the floor, and with whatever you are sitting or lying on. Feel the air touching your skin. Feel your breath.

■ Now see if you can notice that you are thinking. See if you can notice your thoughts as just another thing that you can be aware of. Notice that this is different from what we often do, which is think while failing to notice that we are thinking.

■ Give a simple, one-word label to your thoughts, depending upon their theme. For example, it could be 'worrying', 'planning', or 'remembering'.

In doing this exercise, you might also notice that it is difficult to *just notice* your thoughts for any length of time. Instead, again and again, you will find yourself pulled into your thoughts, before you notice what is happening and step back from them once again. You can practise this exercise often, wherever you are and whatever you are doing – it need not take more than a few moments.

If you want to put aside some dedicated time to learning to notice your thoughts, try this exercise:

Exercise 3.5
Watching and listening

- Sit comfortably, and either close your eyes or lower your gaze.

- Tune into the sensations of breathing, and attend to them for a minute or two, as best you can.

- When you are ready, start to notice what you are thinking. See if it is possible to observe your thoughts, rather than being caught up in them.

■ When your thoughts appear in words, you might find that you can listen to them as though you were hearing them playing on a radio. When they appear in pictures, it might be as though they are images projected onto a screen.

■ You will find that you are frequently pulled back into your stream of thought. You will realise that you are no longer observing or noticing thoughts, but instead are caught up in them, thinking them. That is no problem. Just see if you can step back and observe them as sounds and images once again.

If you practise this exercise regularly, perhaps setting aside some time for it each day, you will become increasingly able to *just notice* your thoughts, instead of getting caught up in them and letting them take control. And you can use it at moments of particular difficulty, when your thoughts are threatening to take control and pull you in unhelpful directions, away from the life that you want to live.

Exercise 3.6

Playing around with thoughts

When you find yourself troubled by anxious thoughts that seem particularly likely to take control of you and pull you away from what you really want to do, you can play around with the 'sound' and 'look' of your thoughts, using this exercise. Of course, while this exercise is playful, we do not mean to suggest that there is anything fun or comic about your anxious thoughts. We know how painful it can be to suffer with anxiety. But this playful technique can be an excellent way to address that serious problem.

- When you notice a particularly troublesome thought, or series of thoughts, in your mind, try repeating it to yourself in a silly voice – perhaps that of a cartoon character, or Darth Vader. Or you could sing it to yourself, perhaps to the tune of 'Happy Birthday'.

- Or you could imagine the thought as a word written out and appearing on a computer screen, in any font or colour, or in neon letters, or in lights that flash on and off.

As you play around with your thoughts in this way, you might find that they start to seem less compelling: less like *you* talking, and more like words produced by your mind. Words that you don't have to buy into or be controlled by.

Exercise 3.7
I'm having the thought that . . .

When you notice yourself having a thought that is liable to take control of you and pull you off-track, simply repeat it to yourself, preceded by the phrase:

'I am having the thought that... [insert your thought here]'.

For example, when Carla found herself bothered by the anxious thought, 'I am going to have a heart attack and traumatise my son', she reminded herself that, 'I am having the thought that... I am going to have a heart attack and traumatise my son'.

This can be a powerful way to remind yourself that your thoughts are just that – thoughts – and so break their spell. When you remember that your thoughts are just thoughts, you have stepped back from them, and are less likely to get caught in a struggle with them or helplessly do what they tell you. They are likely to keep on coming, of course, but that is no problem – the aim is not to get rid of them, after all. So when Carla repeatedly had the thought, 'I am going to have a heart attack and traumatise my son', she used this technique each time it came back, and that enabled her to carry on playing with her son, which is what she really wanted to do.

Exercise 3.8
Thank your mind

Although your mind might bother you at times, remember that it is only trying to help. And so, when it makes a comment or a suggestion that could interfere with what you really want to do, respond to it as you would a friend whose advice you sometimes listen to, and sometimes don't. You could say something like, 'Thanks, Mind. I know you are only trying to help, and I appreciate it, but right now that's not the advice I need.'

Again, this technique is not a way to stop your troublesome thoughts: they are likely to keep on coming. But it can be easier to avoid an exhausting struggle with your mind when you remember what a good friend it is to you, and that, just as with a good friend, you can take its advice on some occasions, and not on others.

Evaluating thoughts for workability

Stepping back from your thoughts gives you the space to decide whether or not engaging with them is likely to be helpful. But isn't that an awful lot like *judging* them? And didn't we tell you in the last chapter that our thoughts are always judging things, and that this can be a problem? So, are we now asking you to judge your own thoughts, just as Carla does in the case example above? Well, yes and no. We are indeed asking you to judge your own thoughts, but in a way that is clear-sighted and takes account of the situation that you are in. That is, instead of being lost in thoughts, some of which are judgements of other thoughts, we can remain fully aware of the present moment and fully aware of what really matters to us in this situation. And then we can decide whether engaging with a particular train of thought will take us in that direction or not. Which is to say, whether or not it is *workable*.

Let's look a bit more closely at Carla's experience, in the example above. She is thinking hard about her thoughts, and whether they are normal, or even perhaps dangerous, and what they might mean. But she has completely lost touch with where she actually is, what she is actually doing, and what matters to her in that situation. Perhaps she is at home, looking after her son. Perhaps she is at work. Perhaps she is on holiday. Wherever she is, it is unlikely that the most useful thing she can do is make an appointment to see her doctor again. And she has lost touch with what really matters to her. It is unlikely that her heart's deepest wish in this moment is really to keep visiting her doctor over and over, to be told over and over again that there is nothing wrong with her. More likely, it is something like connecting positively with her son (if she is with him), or being productive at her job (if she is at work), or exploring new things (if she is on holiday). If she could step back from her thoughts and simply notice them, together with her current situation and the opportunities it affords, she could form a wise judgement about what to do next.

Taking action

This is the crucial point: getting lost in thought is a problem because it affects what we *do*, and, over time, what we do in each moment adds up to the sort of life we have, and the sort of person we are. And so the aim is to free our actions from the control of our thoughts, and direct our actions instead towards what we truly want (we will help you to clarify what you truly want in Chapter 7). In order to do this, we must learn to step back from thoughts and see clearly where they are taking us, but in the end we will have to *take action*, even in the presence of thoughts that tell us that we shouldn't, can't or won't.

Fortunately, this is easier than it might sound, because our thoughts simply have no power to control us, except the power that we give them. They are words and pictures in the mind, and need not direct our behaviour. Don't believe us? Try this:

Exercise 3.9
Your mind cannot control you

- Think to yourself, 'I cannot lift my left arm'. Think it over and over, and really mean it.

- While you are thinking it . . .

- . . . Lift your left arm.

This exercise is not entirely realistic, because you are deliberately producing the thought, 'I can't . . .', but it still applies to real-life situations. If that thought could not control your actions, why is it that other ones do? Only because you believe they must, and don't notice that it is happening. Of course, developing a new habit – of noticing and *not* automatically obeying your thoughts – is going to take time and effort. Don't expect it be easy at first – it might be frightening not to do what your anxious thoughts tell you. But with the understanding that *you*, not your thoughts, control your actions, you can start to move your life in the directions that really matter to you. Let's start right now.

Exercise 3.10
Disobey your thoughts

■ In the next hour, try to disobey one of your thoughts. Do the opposite of what your mind tells you.

■ It can be something very small, such as, 'Reading this book is too hard, I think I'll stop', or, 'Why don't I have a snack?' or even, 'I should keep reading even though I'm tired and need a rest'. It doesn't matter what the thought is – the point is to discover that you don't have to obey it.

■ If you do this often, it will become increasingly clear to you that it is up to *you*, not your thoughts, what actions you take.

A better relationship

Our ability to think is one of our greatest assets... and our greatest burdens. Our brilliant problem-solving minds only want to help us, and they have brought us many great benefits, but they can become a problem for us, because they can generate an endless supply of worries and our worries carry the emotional weight of real threats. Because our thoughts have the power to upset us, we either do what our minds tell us, which can lead us off-track, or we try to control them, seeking to get rid of the 'bad' thoughts and have 'good' ones instead. But we are doomed to fail, because the mind does not have a 'delete' function, and so we use up our energy and attention in fruitless struggle with our anxious thoughts, while our lives pass us by. Fortunately, there is a way out of this trap: we can cultivate a better relationship with our minds by learning to unhook from them. We can learn to step back from our thoughts, see clearly whether or not engaging with them will take us in a direction that we want to go, and then take whatever action we choose, in line with what matters to us. If we can choose when to listen to our brilliant minds and when not to, just as we do with our friends, then everyone wins. We get to live the life that we want, and our minds get to help us do it.

Takeaways
- Remember that much of our thinking is an effort to identify and solve problems.
- Our problem-solving can be a problem because: we can always generate new worries, our worries feel as frightening as real threats, and we cannot delete our thoughts.

■ We can escape from this trap by stepping back from our thoughts, evaluating how useful they are, and deciding how to act based on what we truly care about, instead of what our minds are telling us.

4 Being more than anxiety

As we saw in the last chapter, our relationship to our thoughts is a major source of our difficulties. We think continuously, and we are transfixed by our thoughts. We get pulled in by them, and we buy into them. We *get hooked* by them, and we do what they tell us. And this process causes particular problems because there is one topic that we think about more than any other: *ourselves*. We think about ourselves a very great deal, and we buy into these thoughts fervently. We pick over and over our thoughts about ourselves, refining and elaborating upon them, and in this process they get knitted together into a *story* – a set of ideas about ourselves that explains what we are like, how we got to be that way, and what this means for us. We repeat our story so often to ourselves that we fail to notice that it is a story, and it comes to seem instead like reality – the complete and final truth about ourselves and our lives.

In this chapter, we will explore the consequences of buying into all this storytelling, and what the alternative might be. We will see that the story you tell about yourself might be limiting and distorting your life, and that you have an alternative to seeing yourself that way.

Who are you?

Let's start by exploring who you currently *think* you are:

Exercise 4.1

I am . . .

Complete the following three statements about yourself, in ways that are relevant to your anxiety. For example, you might write down statements about your experience of anxiety, such as, 'I am anxious', or, 'I am a worrier'. And you might write down your worries about yourself, for example, 'I am incompetent', or, 'I am weak':

I am. . .

I am. . .

I am. . .

Now ask yourself, are you *always* those things, in every moment? Are there moments when you are *not* those things? And what if you someday stopped being those things? Would you still be you? The answer, probably, is that these attributes of yours come and go – in some situations you worry, and in others you don't – but that nonetheless they have come to seem like essential, unchanging aspects of who you are. They have come to be a part of your *story* about yourself.

The story of you

The human mind is a master storyteller. It knits thoughts together into narratives: things are like *this* because of *that*, which means that *this* is likely to happen, whereas *that* couldn't possibly. And when we have a good narrative figured out, we feel safe and secure. We know what's going on in a given situation, and we know what to expect. It may be unpleasant to worry all the time about things going wrong, but at least, or so we seem to reason, there are no surprises when it happens.

Our stories, like most of our thinking, are efforts to problem-solve, and the most complex and pressing problem, for many of us, is ourselves and our lives. If we could just understand this complex problem, we imagine, then we could finally be happy. And so we think about ourselves endlessly, and we stitch our thoughts together into a *story* about ourselves. 'I'm like *this*', we tell ourselves, 'because of *that*, which means that *this* is how things are likely to go for me, and I certainly couldn't (or shouldn't) do *that*'. And armed with this account of ourselves, we move through the world, trying to stay safe from dangers and find happiness.

Our self-stories certainly have their uses. Without a thumbnail sketch of who we are, we might not know what to do with ourselves day by day, or how to relate to others. But they can all too easily become a trap when we hold on to them too tightly. When we think we know exactly who we are, what we are like, and what we are capable of, we close off all possibilities that lie outside the bounds of our story.

This is obviously so with our negative stories about ourselves. If we tell ourselves that we are vulnerable, incompetent or incapable of doing certain things, then of course we limit the range of things that we are willing to do. But even positive self-stories are limiting. If we are wedded to a particular positive view of ourselves, then we are liable to feel strongly threatened by anything that could challenge that view, and take steps to avoid it. We may fear to take risks or try new things, and when something comes along that reveals our weaknesses, we may struggle to cope.

If you suffer with anxiety, it is likely that your story about yourself is getting in your way. It may be a negative or a positive story, or it may be both: many of us say both negative and positive things about ourselves, depending on the situation. But whatever its details, it is likely that your reaction to your story sometimes stops you from doing the things that you really want to.

Let's see what your story is:

Exercise 4.2

Who does your story say you are?

■ In this exercise, you will articulate some of your self-story.

■ Spend five minutes writing about yourself, from the perspective of your anxiety.

■ Write about what kind of person you are, what kinds of things you are good at and not good at, what things you can and can't do, and, in particular, what your anxiety stops you from doing.

■ When you have written your story out, give it a name. It can be anything that you like.

For example, Nicole from Chapter 1 called her story 'The incompetence story', and it began like this:

> *I'm not that clever, but I am a hard worker – that is how I have managed to get where I have. And I am a worrier. I think I get that from my mum, but also from all the financial problems that my parents had when I was little. My dad was very irresponsible, and so we often didn't have enough money, and my mum had to keep everything running and keep an eye on everything. I learned that if you don't pay attention to every little detail, something important will slip through the net and you'll find yourself in a serious mess – which was what happened whenever my mum wasn't on top of what my dad was doing. I do wish I could relax and have a bit more confidence in myself, but that's just not the way I am. If I were a bit more of a natural when it comes to staying organised and*

> *getting things done, then maybe I could relax a bit more, and have more time to exercise, see my friends and so on. But unfortunately I'm a bit like my dad in many respects: if I don't work hard to stay on top of things, details slip by me and I can easily get into a muddle, so I can't afford to relax. So I'm anxious like my mum, but disorganised like my dad – what a combination! Although I suppose I should be grateful for the anxiety, as unpleasant as it is, because it keeps the disorganisation in check. Sometimes I don't know where I would be without it.*

As you write your own story, you might find that just writing it down and naming it helps you to *unhook* from it a little and see it as just a story, told by your mind: a sequence of thoughts about yourself that have been repeated many times, and have become very familiar to you. Or it might seem just as true as ever, and you might wonder just how we are going to talk you out of it. Well, we aren't. Your mind knows a lot more about you than we do, and it could probably win any debate on that topic. It has worked hard, over many years, to stitch together your story and collect evidence for it. What we are going to ask you to do, instead, is consider how *workable* your story is: whether dwelling on it and buying into it helps you to live the life that you want to, or whether it gets in your way.

Exercise 4.3

When you listen to your story . . .

- Read over your story and think about it. Allow yourself to believe it – let it really get its teeth into you.

- Ask yourself: when I buy into this story, what do I *do* or *not do*? What actions do I feel unable to take, and what actions do I feel compelled to take?

For example, Nicole wrote down:

> 'When I buy into my story, I spend ages planning, preparing and checking everything, and I don't speak up at work or put myself forward for things. I spend all my time worrying or preparing, and don't have time for the things I enjoy'.

- Then ask yourself: do these actions take me towards or further away from the life that I want?

- Now ask yourself: if this story were *not* my story (or if I didn't buy into it), how differently would I live my life? Write down what you really want to do, but don't do, because you believe in your story.

For instance, Nicole wrote down this:

> *'If I did not buy into this story, I would not spend so much time worrying about things, planning them, preparing for them, and checking that I've done everything right. I would act with more confidence, especially at work, and trust myself to know what to do. I would probably get a lot more done, and would have time to do more stuff that really matters to me, like seeing my friends and exercising. All that worrying, planning, preparing and checking takes up a lot of time!'*

The aim of articulating and naming your story is, of course, to give you greater freedom to *act* in the ways that you truly want to, rather than being controlled by your story. Whenever it threatens to take control, you can unhook from your story simply by acknowledging that it is present, and naming it. As soon as you say, 'Ah, there's The Incompetence Story again' (or whatever the name of your story is), then you have stepped back from it, and might find yourself more able to act freely and do the things that your story says you cannot do.

Or you can aim more directly at that outcome, by simply working out what it is that your story stops you from doing, and *doing it anyway*. For Nicole, this would mean deciding to do her work in a reasonable amount of time, with no more than a reasonable amount of planning, preparing or checking – no matter what the story produced by her mind says about it. For example, she might decide to allocate four hours in total to planning, writing and checking her report, and to use the time that she saves for seeing a friend – something that she truly wants to do. To really emphasise that she, and not her story, is in control, she could even type her story into her phone and keep it with her while she does precisely what it says she must not do: finish her work in a reasonable timeframe and then go and see a friend.

Now for your turn:

Exercise 4.4
When you *don't* listen to your story

■ Think of a specific action that you would like to do, but that your story says that you cannot or should not do.

This does not need to be anything big. In fact, it would be good to pick something small and everyday so that you can do it soon – or even right now.

- Make a plan: where and when will you do it? Could you do it right away?

- Now type your story into your phone (or write it on a piece of paper) and carry it with you in your pocket while you do what it says you cannot or should not do.

In doing this exercise, you might find that you experience anxiety. That is not a problem. Remember that your mind spins your story in an effort to keep things predictable and safe, so we should expect that going beyond your story will feel frightening. But the price of keeping things safe and predictable is that your life will stay the same. If you want things to change in the ways that matter to you, anxiety must inevitably be a part of that process.

When you do what your story says you cannot or must not do, you might discover that it is not, in fact, the last word on who you are and what you are capable of. You might see that your story is made up of words that appear in your mind, which you often allow to weigh you down and control you, but need not.

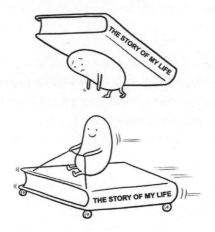

If you are not your story...

When we are hooked by our stories, we view the world *through* them, like a lens through which everything else is filtered, and which we don't even notice is there. Whereas when we start to unhook from them, we look *at* them, and see them as *just stories*, made up of thoughts that come and go. Sometimes our stories are at the forefront of our minds, and sometimes they are not.

If our stories come and go in this way, can they reflect who we truly are? If you are only anxious some of the time, then the statement 'I am anxious' cannot sum you up. If you are not worried every single minute of every day, then there must be more to you than the statement 'I am a worrier'. Even if you *are* anxious or worried all day long, it is unlikely that you are anxious and worried to exactly the same degree all the time. Probably your anxiety and worry are more intense at some times, and less intense at others. And if they change like this, can they really be central to who you are? The real *you* must be something more durable – some aspect of you that is always there, and always has been.

Exercise 4.5
I really am . . .

- Go back to the statements that you wrote in Exercise 4.1, and cross out the parts in each statement that change. For example, in the statement 'I am anxious' the word 'anxious' changes, so it would be crossed out. The same goes for 'a worrier' in the statement, 'I am a worrier'.

- Once you have crossed out the parts of your statements that change, notice what is left in each one. It may only be the words, 'I am . . .'

- Whatever happens, whatever thoughts and feelings come and go, whatever actions you take, there is something that just *is*, and that notices and observes all the rest. That 'something', the awareness that notices everything else come and go, is *you*.

Let's try to see this more clearly, by returning once again to noticing thoughts:

Exercise 4.6
Who notices?

- Sit comfortably, or lie down if you prefer.

- Close your eyes, or if you prefer to leave them open, lower your gaze.

- Tune into the sensations of breathing.

- After a few moments, see if you can notice what you are thinking. See if it is possible to observe your thoughts as though they were images projected onto a screen, or words coming from a radio.

- Now notice that it's *you* that is observing your thoughts, and that if you can observe them, then you cannot also be them.

- Can you connect to this sense of yourself as the observer of all your changing experiences, including the stories produced by your mind?

- Whenever you realise that you are no longer observing your train of thought, but instead have got pulled into it, just return to observing – to noticing.

Probably, in doing this exercise, you spent most of your time lost in your thoughts, just *thinking*, rather than observing your thoughts. But perhaps there were a few moments when you were *aware* of what you were thinking, and were able to notice that it seemed to be *you* that was doing this observing (who else could it be, after all?). But then awareness dwindled, you got caught up in thinking once again, and the sense of being separate from your thoughts disappeared.

The perspective from which you can notice your story, and all of your other thoughts (and your feelings, and anything else), is the perspective of present-moment awareness. It is always available to you, as a truer, more stable sense of self than the one offered by your story about yourself. Instead of being 'anxious', 'a worrier', or anything else that your mind might call you, you are the awareness that notices and contains all these thoughts (together with feelings, sights, sounds, smells and tastes). This awareness is always there, unchanging, distinct from your thoughts and feelings, and it always has been, just as the sky is always there, holding the weather that moves across it.

Exercise 4.7 (Adapted from Sinclair & Beadman, 2016)

A mind like the sky

- If you are able to, look at the sky. Or if you are not, imagine the sky.

■ Notice what you can see against the backdrop of the sky: sun or moon, clouds or clear blue, rain or snow, birds and planes.

■ Notice how they move and change. Even the sun and moon are slowly moving across the sky. Even the blue or grey of the sky is slowly changing, and by nightfall will turn to black.

■ Now find a comfortable seat and close your eyes or, if you prefer to leave them open, lower your gaze.

■ Notice your thoughts, taking shape and moving across your mind, like clouds across the sky.

■ Notice your feelings, changing more slowly, like the weather patterns that cover the whole sky but never stay the same.

■ Notice the awareness that contains your thoughts and feelings, like the sky that contains, but is not changed by, whatever passes across it.

■ Notice that *you* are that awareness.

When we take up the perspective of awareness, instead of that of our stories and other thoughts, we can find stability and freedom. We discover that we are more than the thoughts, emotions, sensations and actions that make up 'anxiety'. We are the awareness that contains them. We realise that our thoughts and feelings cannot hurt us or change who we truly are. Awareness is always there, unchanging, however anxious we may get – it always has been, and it always will be. From this perspective, we can learn to stay steady in the face of anxiety. Seeing that we need not be pulled this way and that by passing thoughts and moods, we can instead remain focused on the more durable, consistent sources of meaning that give our lives vitality and purpose (more on this in Chapter 7). From the perspective of awareness, it becomes possible to notice thoughts and feelings and to *choose* how to respond to them, in line with what truly matters to us.

And from the perspective of awareness, we need never feel alone. The stories that we tell about ourselves are, in large part, efforts to find our place in the world – I am like *this* and you are like *that*, and so *this* is how we should relate to each other. But all too often they serve instead to isolate us from others. They tell us that we do not belong and cannot connect with others, or that we need to be better in order to win their respect. But from the perspective that we have been exploring here, we all share common ground: the ground of awareness. Everyone has thoughts and feelings that come and go, everyone struggles and suffers, and everyone is *aware* of all this. Everyone, we could say, truly *is* that awareness. From the perspective of awareness, we are all alike, and so none of us need feel alone. And from the perspective of awareness, perhaps we can respond with kindness to our suffering, and with a sincere wish to relieve it. Perhaps we can respond with *compassion* – more of this in Chapter 6.

Exercise 4.8
Unchanging awareness
(Adapted from Hayes et al. 1999)

- Take up a comfortable position and either close your eyes or lower your gaze.

- Tune into the sensations of breathing and spend a minute or two gently attending to them.

- When you are ready, bring to mind a somewhat painful memory from your childhood. Note that it should only be 'somewhat' painful – don't go for the worst thing that you can remember.

- Try to remember the thoughts and feelings that you had at the time. Notice also the sights, sounds and smells in the memory.

- Notice that if you can notice these things, then you cannot *be* them. Notice that the part of you that notices them does not change, and never has. It is the same today as it was back then.

- Now think of a somewhat painful memory from the more recent past. Again, recall your thoughts and feelings in the memory, and the sights, sounds and smells. Again, notice that you are more than those experiences. You are the faculty of *awareness* that noticed them then and notices them now. Notice that it has not changed.

- Now notice your thoughts and feelings in this moment, and the sounds and smells around you. Again, notice that if you can notice these things then you cannot *be* them. Notice that you are aware of them, and that this is the same awareness that you have had all your life. Notice that it does not change, no matter what passes through it.

■ What would it mean to *be* this awareness? And what would it mean if everyone else was awareness, too?

In doing this exercise, you might have noticed the stability of your awareness through time. Thoughts and feelings have come and gone, but the awareness that notices them did not change. You can practise seeing things from this perspective – the perspective of awareness – by doing this exercise frequently. And in any moment when thoughts and feelings threaten to pull you off track, you can connect with the perspective of awareness to find greater stability and freedom to act as you choose to.

Being yourself

Much of the time, we are so hooked by our thoughts that they create our reality, and this is never more so than when we are thinking about our favourite subject: *ourselves*. Each of us has a story about ourselves that we have repeated so often that it has come to seem like the unarguable truth. But these stories, though useful up to a point, become traps when we hold onto them too tightly. They tell us what we can and cannot do, and hold us back from the lives that we truly want to live. And so, if you feel like anxiety is in control of your life, then it might be time to start unhooking from your story about yourself.

When we begin to loosen our grip on our stories – and their grip on us – we can start to discover who we really are: the awareness that contains our thoughts (including our stories), our feelings, and everything else that we are aware of. As the contents of our awareness come and go, never standing still, awareness itself does not change. It has always been there, and always will be, larger than our anxiety and untouched by it. When we adopt the perspective of awareness, it is possible to stand back from whatever is happening in any given moment. We can take a broader view, find stability and make wise choices, rather than being yanked around by the thoughts and feelings of that moment. And we can know that we are not alone, because everyone else, like us, is really this expansive, unchanging awareness.

Takeaways

■ Remember that we all have a story about ourselves – a narrative that says who we are, what we are like, and what we can and cannot do.

■ While these stories can be useful, we often hold on to them too tightly, and let them hold us back from doing the things that matter to us.

■ You are more than the story that your mind tells about you. You are the awareness that contains everything that you are aware of: your thoughts, your feelings, your story and everything else.

■ This awareness is larger than what it contains, is always the same, and is the same for everyone.

■ When you take up the perspective of awareness, you can find the stability and wisdom to do what matters to you, regardless of what your story says you can or cannot do.

5

Being willing

In Chapter 3, we looked at how our thoughts can cause problems for us, because we tend to either struggle against them or be controlled by them. And we highlighted a crucial reason why we do this: because our thoughts *feel* like something, and so they motivate us to take action, in order to feel better. But as we have seen, while they might make us feel better in the short term, such actions often have costs over the longer term. And so in this chapter, we ask two radical questions:

■ *What if we don't need to feel better? And,*

■ *If we stopped devoting our time and energy to trying to feel better, what might we do instead?*

Feeling better

It is natural to want to feel better. In fact, you could say that that is what feelings – both emotions and body sensations – are *for*. They are signals that alert us to what is good or bad for us; what we should move towards or away from. Think again of our proto-human ancestor who fashioned the first spear. Like us, they wanted to feel pleasure and avoid pain, and their feelings pointed them in the direction of what was good for them. Eating felt good, hunger felt bad; being accepted by their tribe felt good, being cast out felt bad. And we are no different today: we are built to respond to our emotions and body sensations, which are continually signalling to us that some things are good for us and should be approached, whereas other things are bad and should be avoided. Winning the lottery feels good, whereas going bankrupt feels bad.

Thinking and feeling

But things are more complicated than that, again because of our amazing ability to think. As we saw in Chapter 3, our feelings don't just show up in response to actual, real-life events, but also in response to our own thoughts. So we can feel afraid when there is nothing to be afraid of, or sad when nothing bad has happened.

And because our minds can link anything to anything, we can manage to feel afraid in pretty much any situation. Having been told that 'bears live in the woods', our cave-dwelling ancestor might feel a twinge of fear when they go into the woods to hunt – and this might help them to stay alert. But what if their mind tries to help them out by suggesting other places where bears might roam? It might say, 'What if there's one by the river?', and, 'What if there's one outside my cave, waiting to ambush me?' They might imagine in vivid detail what it would be like to be attacked by a bear. They would feel fear each time they contemplated going to the river or even leaving their cave, and the only way to make it stop would be to stay in their cave, where they felt safe. In trying to feel better, in trying to avoid the painful feeling of fear, they might give up doing the things that mattered to them.

Feelings as threats

And it gets worse, because our clever thinking minds often label our thoughts and feelings *themselves* as 'bad' or 'dangerous'. If something feels painful, as fear and worry do, then we are motivated to avoid it, and if we avoid it, then we infer that it must be dangerous. And so, as well as trying to head off the disasters that we fear, we get caught in struggle with our thoughts and feelings *themselves*, trying to avoid them or make them go away. We have already discussed our struggles with our thoughts. Our struggles with our feelings are equally fruitless. We might feel angry with our feelings, as though they were deliberately persecuting us. We might be fearful of them, worrying that our anxiety will cause us harm, or is a signal that something is wrong with us. We might try to suppress them, or to distract ourselves from them, or to stop them arising in the first place by avoiding whatever triggers them. Look back at how you filled in the table in Exercise 1.1, in Chapter 1, to see some of the ways that you struggle with your painful feelings.

None of these strategies work very well, as we saw in Exercise 1.1, Chapter 1. When we are angry with or fearful of our painful feelings, we are just layering more anguish on top of them (if you are fearful of your fear, then you just wind up twice as afraid). And when we try to suppress them, avoid them or distract ourselves from them, it never works for long, and our efforts pull us away from the things that we really care about and undermine our quality of life. Suppression takes energy that you need for other, more satisfying things. Distraction is, well, distracting – if you surf the internet all day, for example, in order to manage your anxiety, you will have little time for more meaningful activities. And if you are determined to avoid situations that might trigger painful thoughts and feelings, then you will have to avoid most of what is meaningful in life. Because – and this is the key point – *discomfort is part of the entry fee for a meaningful life*.

Pain is not the enemy

Attempts to get rid of painful feelings are so corrosive to a meaningful life because pain shows up in precisely the areas that matter most to us. Consider the areas of your life in which you get most anxious. Are they unimportant to you? Do you get anxious about things that don't matter? Probably not. We get anxious in precisely the situations that we care about, because in them we have the most to gain and the most to lose. Our problem-solving minds go into overdrive, seeking to identify and address every possible thing that could go wrong. And so we become anxious and, all too often, get lost in struggle with our feelings, or turn away from the very situations that we care about, in order to relieve our distress. We allow our anxiety to keep us from what we care about, and over time our lives become constricted and empty.

Let's have a look at an example:

Amir can feel how nervous he is. He can feel the adrenaline in his system, and the tightness in his throat. He hates this feeling like a personal enemy. For as long as he can remember, it's been with him, showing up whenever he least wants it to, and turning him into an awkward, stammering wreck. He knows just what's going to happen: he's going to go all quiet, and choke on his words when he tries to speak, and Zeina's friends are going to think he's a loser, and then *she's* going to think he's a loser too, and probably she won't want to go out with him anymore. He feels another jolt of fear, and his throat tightens further, and he thinks how stupid he was to agree to meeting her friends this soon, when he knew perfectly well what would happen. He feels so frustrated and angry with himself that he wants to scream or punch himself in the face, but instead he just clenches his fists tighter, trying to crush this stupid feeling. 'Are you okay?' Zeina asks him, and he just grunts and nods, feeling too upset to speak. 'Are you sure you want to go?' she asks him. 'You don't have to'. For a moment, he feels blessed relief – he could just *not go*. His throat relaxes, and his stomach settles. But he couldn't do that, he thinks, and so he tells her that, no, he wants to go. But his anxiety revs higher again, and he feels his stomach knot. God it's awful. And it's going to go wrong, he just knows it. He's not good with groups, and this isn't going to be any different. Maybe he really *shouldn't* go, he thinks, and again feels a moment of relief. Maybe he should tell Zeina that he's tired, and maybe it's not the best time, and he doesn't want to drag the evening down, so she should go alone.

When Zeina says that it's time to set off, he feels a horrible wave of dread, and finds himself saying that, actually, maybe he should just go home after all, as he's really tired and won't be much fun. 'Okay', Zeina says, and he asks if that's alright, and she says, yes, of course it is. But her tone is kind of abrupt.

In this example, Amir is confronted with a situation that matters to him: meeting his new girlfriend's friends, hopefully making a good impression on them, and thus strengthening his connection with her. But because the situation matters to him, his mind, trying to help, comes up with its usual, habitual predictions of disaster, and he feels intensely anxious. Not only is the anxiety unpleasant, but it seems like a threat in and of itself. Amir's mind comes up with a story about how his anxiety itself will cause a problem, and he feels furious with it and with himself, and tries unsuccessfully to suppress it. All of which just amplifies his distress. And while he is caught up in this struggle with his feelings, he is unable to do what matters to him: to connect in a positive way with his girlfriend. When he is offered a way out – the possibility of going home – his anxiety eases and he feels sweet relief. And ultimately this proves too tempting. Faced with a choice between anxiety and relief, he cannot resist the latter, and so he tells his girlfriend that he is going home. She seems a little upset. And so, because he was not able to bear with his anxiety, Amir has taken a step away from what mattered to him in this situation: nurturing the connection between him and his girlfriend.

What might Amir have done differently, and what might we all do differently when faced with anxiety? We can stop treating anxiety as something dangerous, a problem to be solved, and start treating it as what it is: just a feeling, that cannot harm us and just might be signalling that we are going in the right direction. We can be willing to have our feelings and take them with us as we travel in the directions that matter to us.

Why be willing?

This might not sound terribly appealing. Who, after all, wants to feel anxiety, if they can avoid it? The answer is: no one does, but the cost of avoiding anxiety is giving up on the life that you want, and we suffer more when we struggle against it. Struggling with your feelings is like holding a beach ball underwater: it takes up your time and energy, it's distracting, and it stops you from doing anything else, such as enjoying your swim. And as soon as you relax your efforts, it will just pop up again. Would you not get more out of your swim if you stopped pushing down on the beach ball and were willing to let it bob around in the water with you? It might get in your way now and again, but nowhere near as much as the effort required to keep it underwater. And similarly, might it not be better, in the end, to be willing to have your feelings, so that you can get on with the things that matter to you?

To decide whether or not you want to develop willingness in relation to your anxiety, try this exercise.

Exercise 5.1
Two sides of a coin

■ Think of two or three situations that make you especially anxious.

■ Write down your answers to the following questions (we have included Amir's answers as an example):

- *In what areas of your life does anxiety show up?*
  For example, Amir answered this question by saying, 'Socialising'.

- *If you were to disengage from those areas of your life, what would you lose that matters to you?*
  Amir's answer was, 'Social connection'.

- *If you could make room for this anxiety, rather than struggling against it, what would that enable you to do in these areas of your life?*
  Amir said, 'I could meet more people, talk to them, and act in a way that is friendly and open. I could make more friends, strengthen the friendships that I have, and strengthen my relationship with my girlfriend.'

Perhaps in answering these questions yourself, you noticed that your anxiety shows up in precisely the parts of your life that matter most to you. Caring and hurting are two sides of the same coin, and so avoiding pain often means giving up what matters most to you in life. If this doesn't seem to apply to you, then that is fine – perhaps your anxiety is not causing such a problem for you after all. But we would guess that if you are reading this book, then your struggle with anxiety is probably getting in the way of living the life that you want to live, and being the person you want to be. And so you may be interested to read on, and try the exercises that follow.

How to be willing

First, let's be clear what we are talking about. Being willing to have your anxiety does not mean tolerating it, teeth gritted. Nor does it mean giving up and resigning yourself to it because you feel that you have no choice. Rather, it means actively opening up to it and turning towards it, saying 'Yes' to it in the knowledge that it is an integral part of the path to a better life.

That might all sound very inspiring, but still, you may ask, how on earth do we *do* it? How do we move from our natural posture of aversion to our anxiety to one of willingness? Well, fortunately we have a few techniques to offer, all of which will help you to:

- See beyond your mind's labelling of anxiety as 'bad' or 'dangerous'.

- Experience it as it really is: just a feeling that is neither 'good' nor 'bad', and is certainly not dangerous.

- Discover that you can stay in contact with it, without anything terrible happening.

- Discover that it is part of the path towards the things that matter to you.

- And even develop a friendlier relationship to it – it's just trying to keep you safe, after all.

Let's start by exploring the relationship between anxiety and the body.

Anxiety in the body

All of our emotions are physical as well as mental experiences. If we pay close attention, we can notice their signatures in the body. For example, sadness might feel like a sinking in the chest or the pit of the stomach, whereas joy might feel like a spreading effervescence. Some people feel these signatures very strongly, whereas others may not be able to notice them without practice. Most of us can notice the physical experience of anxiety, though, because it shows up particularly strongly, being linked to the fight-or-flight response, which we introduced in Chapter 1. We are all familiar with the sensations of a pounding heart and butterflies in the stomach, and for many of us, as for Amir in the example above, this is one of the most unpleasant aspects of anxiety.

But what, actually, is so bad about these sensations? They cannot harm us (no one has ever fainted, had a heart attack, or lost their mind due to anxiety – despite what our minds might tell us). And under other circumstances we don't even experience them as unpleasant. Heart pounding and rapid breathing? That happens when we run for the bus. Adrenaline and butterflies in the stomach? That could be the feeling of falling in love. The unpleasantness of the sensations of anxiety is in part due to how we interpret them, that is, the story that our mind is telling about them.

To see this more clearly, and start to re-interpret your anxiety, try this:

Exercise 5.2
Jump around

- Do some physical activity, right now, such as running on the spot or jumping up and down, until you are out of breath.

- Now tune into your body sensations. Notice how your heart feels. Notice your breathing. Notice the overall sense of energy and agitation in your body.

- If you felt these sensations in a situation in which you normally get anxious, what would you make of them? Would they seem pleasant, neutral, or unpleasant? Would you be happy to have them, or would you want them to go away?

Perhaps, in doing this exercise, you noticed that the body sensations of anxiety are not unique to anxiety, and they are not, in themselves, terribly unpleasant. Rather, it is the mind's interpretation of them as 'bad' or 'dangerous' that makes them so. Next time you feel anxious, you might want to reflect upon this.

To take this process further, we can explore the bodily sensations of anxiety by paying close attention to them. In doing so, we can go beyond the mind's tendency to label these sensations as 'bad', 'dangerous' and 'to be avoided'. Instead we can come to see them as harmless, and even as interesting. (And if your mind tries to talk you out of exploring your anxiety in this way, take another look at 'Why be willing'? above, to remind yourself of why it might be worthwhile.)

Exercise 5.3

Beyond good and bad
(Adapted from Harris, 2008)

- Close your eyes or let your gaze rest softly on a still spot in front of you.

- Focus your attention on a part of your body that feels pretty neutral – perhaps the soles of your feet, or your hands, or your bottom on the seat. You can return your attention here at any point during the exercise if you start to feel overwhelmed.

- Now let go of that focus of attention and call to mind an issue that you feel a bit anxious about. Just a bit anxious – don't go for the worst thing in your life. Let it come into your mind and spend a few moments thinking about this anxiety-provoking situation.

- Now, direct your attention to the body.

- Notice any body sensations that are part of your emotional reaction to this issue (for example, you might notice your heart beating fast, butterflies in your stomach, or tightness in your throat).

■ Explore one of these sensations with an attitude of curiosity, as if you were a curious scientist discovering the sensation for the very first time.

For example:

- If you were able to draw an outline around the sensation, what shape would it take?

- Notice whether the sensation sits at the surface of your body or goes deeper inside, and, if so, notice how deep.

- What is the temperature of the sensation? Does it feel warm or cool?

- How about the weight of the sensation – is it light or heavy?

- If the sensation had a texture, what would that be? Is it smooth or rough on its surface?

- Is the sensation moving or changing? Perhaps it is vibrating, or pulsing, or is still.

■ Notice how you are responding to the sensation. You might want it to go away, you might be trying to suppress it, or you might be tightening your muscles around it.

- See if it is possible to just let the sensation be there.

  - You could try relaxing any muscles that you are tensing.

  - You could try breathing into the area where the difficult sensation is, and imagining that with each in-breath, you create space within you for the sensation, and with each out-breath you breathe out your resistance to the sensation.

  - You could say to yourself, 'It's okay, let me feel this', or, 'I don't have to like this but it's okay for it to be here', or whatever words help you to connect with an attitude of acceptance.

  - You could remind yourself of why you want to accept this sensation – that you are trying to move towards the things that you truly care about.

- Notice that there is more to you than these feelings. Notice that the *you* that is noticing them must be separate from and larger than them.

- When you are ready, open your eyes.

What happened when you did this exercise? Perhaps your anxious feeling went away, or perhaps it stayed the same, or perhaps it intensified. All of these outcomes are perfectly good, because the aim of the exercise is not to change or get rid of your anxious feelings, but rather to relate to them differently. And perhaps, in doing this exercise, you got some sense of what that might mean. Perhaps you noticed that your anxious feelings are just feelings, and that they cannot harm you, no matter what your mind might say about them. Perhaps you got some sense of what it would be like to just let your anxious feelings be there, without trying to figure them out or make them go away. Perhaps you can imagine being willing to take them with you, as you move towards the life you want.

Do not wait for the most painful feelings to show up before practising this exercise. You can practise with all sorts of feelings, whether mild or strong, pleasant or unpleasant, and we recommend that you do so. If you practise often, with all kinds of feelings, then you can cultivate a whole new relationship with your feelings. You can watch them come and go like the weather moving across the sky. You can savour the pleasant and accept the painful, while remaining oriented towards what truly matters to you.

When it's all too much

As powerful as it can be to 'turn towards' your anxiety by exploring it in the body, sometimes it is just not possible. The storm of thoughts and feelings may be so intense that it sweeps you away, and you may find yourself lost in a vortex of anxiety, unable to remain connected to the present moment and to do the things that you want to. At such times you need something different: a way of staying rooted in the here-and-now; grounded in the present moment. Try this simple grounding exercise:

Exercise 5.4

Keep your feet on the ground
(Adapted from Harris, 2019)

■ In the midst of whatever you are doing, simply place your feet flat on the floor and tune into the sensations at their soles. You might like to press your feet into the floor a few times to feel the floor beneath you.

■ Now relax and notice whatever you feel at the soles of your feet. You might notice sensations of touch. You might notice warmth or coolness, or numbness. Just notice whatever you can feel there.

■ Whenever you notice that your mind has wandered off, perhaps into worrying, just acknowledge the thoughts and feelings, maybe saying to yourself, 'Here's worry', or, 'Here's anxiety', and then bring your attention back to the soles of the feet.

■ Notice that along with any worry or fear that may be here, your body is also here, containing these painful experiences; a body that you can move and control.

■ There is no need to maintain total, unbroken attention to the soles of the feet. Just remain aware of them to whatever extent allows you to stay grounded in the present moment while you re-engage with what matters to you, right here and right now.

■ If you prefer, you can use other body sensations for this technique – you could feel the palms of the hands, or the breath, or your body resting on your seat. Experiment, and see what works for you.

While doing this exercise, you might notice that your thoughts and feelings quieten down, or even stop. While that might be welcome, it is not the point of the exercise. The point is not to distract yourself from thoughts and feelings, but rather to stay in the present moment, allowing thoughts and feelings to come and go, while you do what matters to you. If you practise this technique often then it can become a strong habit. You might find that you can remain gently aware of the soles of the feet (or some other body sensation) for large parts of your day. And then when things get really intense, and you struggle to stay on track in the face of strong emotions, you can simply connect strongly with the soles of the feet, and use them as an anchor point to help you stay steady and resolute in pursuing the life that you want.

Just do it!

Ultimately, the problem with your anxious feelings is not that you have them, or that they are unpleasant, but that you let them stop you from doing the things that matter to you. Fortunately, that is a problem that you can solve. By *just doing* the things that matter to you, even in the presence of anxiety, you can discover that your anxiety can be a part of, rather than an obstacle to, a life full of meaning and fulfilment. As you do this, you will find yourself increasingly willing to have your anxiety, rather than merely tolerating it, as you do what matters to you. Your mind will be less inclined to label anxiety as a bad thing to be avoided, and more as an integral part of a life well-lived.

We will be going into this in a lot more detail in Chapter 7, but we can start work on it right away. So let's try it:

Exercise 5.5
Ready, willing, go!

Think of something that you would really like to do, but that makes you feel anxious. Think of an action you could take that is clear, specific and definitely doable. For example, Amir might have a goal of attending a social event with his girlfriend. Then take that action, and fill in a table like the one below, which we have filled in with an example from Amir.

In your table, record the following information:

■ Why you chose to take this action.

Try to connect with the heartfelt wish that motivates you.

■ The thoughts and feelings that showed up while you took your chosen action.

These are likely to be obstacles that often stop you from doing the things that you want to.

■ Any techniques that you used to manage your thoughts and feelings.

You might make use of any of the techniques that you have learned so far in this book.

■ Your degree of willingness to experience your anxiety, scoring it from 1 to 10, where 1 is 'not at all willing' and 10 is 'completely willing'.

Note that you are *not* scoring your willingness to take your chosen action, but rather your willingness to feel your anxiety as you do so. And note that there is no expectation that your anxiety will reduce during the activity – that is not the aim of the exercise. Rather, the aim is to track and cultivate your *willingness* to feel your anxiety, so that you can do the things that matter to you.

Meaningful action	Why do this?	What thoughts, emotions and body sensations showed up?	Techniques I used to manage unpleasant thoughts, emotions and body sensations	My degree of willingness to experience my anxiety (1-10)
Coffee with one of Zeina's friends	Because I care about connection and our relationship	**Thoughts** I'm going to make a fool of myself **Emotions** Anxiety, shame **Body sensations** Pounding heart, tightness in throat, butterflies in stomach	**Present-moment awareness and flexible attention** Noticing sights, sounds, colours and sensations **Unhooking from thoughts** I'm having the thought that . . . **Opening up to anxiety** Beyond good and bad; Keep your feet on the ground	6

Once you have done this with one action, think of some more, and keep on going. For example, Amir could attend a range of social events, and he could start to think of other types of situations that make him anxious and work on those as well. Remember to keep on tracking your level of willingness to feel your anxiety, and don't worry if it goes up and down – that is normal. Over time, you can develop increased willingness to feel anxiety, in the knowledge that it is an integral part of doing the things that make life meaningful.

Turning towards anxiety

We all want to feel good, and this is only natural. The whole reason that we *have* feelings is to motivate us to move towards what is good for us, and away from what is bad for us. But this system often does not work in our best interests, because of the complexities of human language and thought. Our clever minds can imagine any number of threats, regardless of whether anything bad is actually happening to us, or is likely to. Because our thoughts trigger our emotions, we feel anxious. Wanting to feel better, we try to problem-solve these imagined threats by worrying, planning, and avoiding the situations in which we think they are likely to show up. We even experience our anxious thoughts and feelings *themselves* as threatening, and get into fruitless struggles with them, trying to suppress them or make them go away, or avoiding anything that could trigger them. Unfortunately, all of this has a dire cost, because our anxiety tends to appear precisely in the areas of our lives that matter most to us. Gripped by the fear of failure, we find ourselves overtaken by anxious thinking and efforts to avoid disaster. And these often, unfortunately, keep us from moving forwards in the areas that we truly care about. The way out of our predicament is simple: we need to be willing to have all of our feelings, including our anxiety, as we take the actions that move us towards the life that we want to live.

Takeaways

- Remember that it is natural to want to avoid pain, but often our efforts to avoid anxiety take us away from what we care about.
- This is because our minds can conjure up anxiety just by thinking, and tend to generate the most anxiety about the situations that matter most to us.
- By cultivating willingness to experience anxiety, in the interests of living a meaningful life, we can take the actions that will move us towards that life.

6 Treating your-self kindly

If you suffer with anxiety, you are probably quite hard on yourself. You might criticise yourself for being anxious and not able to cope with things. Or you might be very hard on yourself when things go wrong. You might even believe that this is a good idea – that it helps you to stay motivated and get things done. In this chapter, we will suggest that being hard on yourself is not always the best way to get things done, and we will offer an alternative. We want to recommend a new way to motivate yourself and deal with the challenges that arise as you do the things that matter to you: an attitude of *compassion*. With compassion, everything becomes easier, including the steps that we are asking you to take in this book.

What is compassion?

Compassion is about relieving suffering. It means acknowledging our difficulties and our imperfections and relating to them with kindness, rather than ignoring them, trying to hide them, or criticising ourselves for having them. It means recognising that we are not alone: everyone has difficulties and imperfections, and so ours unite us with the rest of humanity, rather than setting us apart. And it means acting in a kind and caring way, towards ourselves and others, in the interests of relieving suffering.

Why compassion?

Compassion is a part of human nature, and one that we cannot do without. For hundreds of thousands of years, we have depended on one another for care and support, and cared for our children. Think again of our cave-dwelling ancestor, whom we met in previous chapters. They would have lived a in a close-knit group, without whom they could not have survived, and they would have depended upon them at times of difficulty and distress. Their children would have been helpless, just like ours today, and utterly dependent upon their caregivers for their survival. Without the capacity to notice and attend to one another's distress, our ancestor, their children, and the rest of the tribe could never have survived.

Compassion, then, is wired deeply into our bodies and brains, and a growing body of scientific evidence is revealing how essential it is for our health and wellbeing. In our modern world, with its advanced technologies and complex societies, we may no longer need care and connection to survive, but we still need them to thrive.

Among many other benefits, compassion can provide us with the sense of stability and safety that we need to push forwards with making positive changes to our lives. When we feel cared for, we have the confidence to explore new territory and to try new things, and the courage to persist in the face of difficulty. Whereas when we feel alone or harshly judged (including by our own minds), we feel vulnerable and under threat. Anxiety increases, and we fall back on our usual anxious habits: we hide from new challenges, or engage in frantic activity, trying to neutralise all possible threats. Compassion, then, is crucial for moving beyond the control of anxiety, and building the life you want.

Two teachers

We can see the usefulness of compassion by thinking about others who have helped us to learn and progress:

Exercise 6.1
The good teacher

- Think of times when you have had to learn things, and of the teachers you have had.

- Remember how effective these teachers were and what it was like to be taught by them. Which ones got the very best of you, and kept you interested in what you were learning, so that you kept at it?

- What qualities did they have? Specifically, how kind and encouraging, as opposed to harsh and critical, were they?

- Now take some time to reflect on the ideal teacher. How would they balance gentleness and toughness, criticism and encouragement? How would they communicate? What tone of voice, posture, and facial expression would they have?

In thinking about your past teachers, you might conclude that a very harsh, unforgiving and critical teacher will not get the best results. In the short term, we might work hard in order to avoid further criticism. But because our focus is on getting *away* from a threat rather than moving *towards* what we want, we are liable to be in fight-or-flight mode, which means that we lack creativity, clear-sightedness and flexibility. We run in circles, doing whatever keeps us safe from attack in the short term, but missing the bigger picture. And over the longer term we are liable to become demoralised and give up on whatever we are trying to learn. In the end, we will seek to escape from our threatening, hectoring teacher by disengaging.

A kind and encouraging teacher, meanwhile, creates a sense of safety and connection. We are confident that we will still be accepted and supported when we fail. This gives us the confidence to take on challenges, to try new things, and to keep on trying even when things don't work out. With a kind and supportive teacher, we make more progress towards the life we want, and find more satisfaction in doing so.

As we discussed in Chapters 3 and 5, our thoughts feel real, and have the same emotional impact as real events. And so, although our minds only want to help, when they try to motivate us with harshness and criticism, it is like being bullied by a harsh and critical teacher. Whereas relating to ourselves with care and kindness is the same as being encouraged and supported by a caring teacher. With compassion for ourselves, we can keep on moving in the directions that we want to go.

Exercise 6.2
What kind of teacher do you have?

■ Think of a project in your life that really matters to you. It could be something that you are already trying to do, or something that you are not already doing but would like to. For example, learning a new skill or building up your social life.

■ What are some of the more self-critical things that you say to yourself when trying to do this thing that matters to you, or when you contemplate doing it? Perhaps things like: 'This is going to go wrong; I always get everything wrong.' 'I'm too anxious for this; I should stick to things that I can cope with.' Or 'Come on, you idiot! Try harder!'

■ What effect do these words have on you? Do they perhaps make you feel anxious or frustrated? Do they make you more or less likely to begin this project or continue with it?

■ What, instead, would you say to yourself if you were a kind and supportive teacher, who really cared about you and wanted what was best for you? Perhaps something like. 'It's understandable that you find this difficult and feel anxious. Just do your best, and if it doesn't work out, that's okay. I'm here to support you and to help you try again'.

■ Could you say these (or similar) words to yourself?

■ To help you come up with some supportive, encouraging words, think of what you might say to someone who you care about – perhaps a good friend – who was finding it difficult to learn a new skill. Now say these words to yourself.

■ Notice what effect these words have on you. How motivated do you feel to continue?

Compassion in action

In doing the exercise above, you might have started to get a sense of how compassion could help you to do the things that you truly want to. Let's have a look at an example, to see in more detail how this works.

Carla has a tremendous amount to do, and not enough time. If she doesn't get everything ready, the party will be a total failure, and the other parents will think that she just doesn't care. They already think she's weird, with all her worrying about her health, and they probably think it has a bad effect on her son. And they're probably right! She feels exhausted, but now is not the time to rest. Who cares how you feel, she tells herself – this needs doing!

She is worried that it won't be good for her, to keep on running around when she is so tired, and she thinks of her heart, with a stab of fear, but this just makes her angry with herself. No one else makes such a fuss, she thinks; she really needs to grow up. Why can't she just *unhook* from all these stupid thoughts, like she has been reading about in *The Little Anxiety Workbook*? She stops for a moment, and tries one of the techniques that she has been reading about, but then isn't sure she is doing it right, and curses herself for being such an idiot that she can't even remember how to do the things that might help her. She gives up and goes back to cleaning the kitchen frantically – if any of the children get ill after the party, it will be her fault. Why can't she ever do anything *right*, she thinks, and feels so upset that she throws the cloth into the sink, sits down in a chair and cries. It's all too much, she thinks. She can't cope. She might as well just go back to bed.

Her phone rings – it's her friend Judy. She is tempted not to pick up, because she feels like such a mess and a loser, but she does. Judy can hear that she is upset and listens as she pours out her worries about the party, and how tired she is, and how it seems as though she can't ever do anything right. She knows that Judy understands about this kind of thing – she was quite depressed a few months ago. And so Judy is able to reassure Carla that it's normal to feel this way, given all the pressure she is under, and when Carla says that no one else gets into this kind of a state, Judy says that everyone has their own problems, many people get anxious, and everyone gets into a state sometimes. Remember how Judy herself was, not so long ago? This helps, and Carla starts to talk Judy through everything that she has to do. You can do it, Judy says, but also you need to rest, and together they figure out which bits really do need doing and which can be put aside, and they make a plan. It all seems much more manageable now. They say goodbye, and Carla hangs up. She does a couple of exercises from *The Little Anxiety Workbook*, to help prepare her for what she needs to do, and then she is ready to begin.

In this example, Carla is caught in a vicious cycle of anxiety and self-attack. The more anxious she feels, the more her mind insults and criticises her, and the more it does that, the more upset and anxious she becomes. Her mind is filled with possible disasters and rules about what she *must* do, and she struggles to remain focussed on what truly matters to her in this situation: an enjoyable party for her son.

She tries to escape through frantic activity, hoping that if she can do everything that her mind tells her, then it will leave her alone. She tries to make use of the techniques that she has learned in this book, but her mind begins to bully her for not remembering them perfectly. Eventually, she cannot sustain her efforts, and gives up and sits down in tears. Organising the party has become such an ordeal that she just wants to disengage from it altogether.

But then Judy calls her, and things take a turn for the better. With Judy's support and encouragement, Carla's sense of being under threat eases, and she is able to see that her situation is not so unusual, shameful or unmanageable. She finds the strength and resolve to re-engage with the situation and do what matters: to focus on what is needed to give her son a party that he will enjoy.

We may not always have a good friend on hand to counsel us through difficult times, but fortunately we can learn to be a good friend to ourselves. If we can learn to relate to ourselves in the way that Judy relates to Carla, then compassion for ourselves can be available in any moment, and can help us to meet challenges and keep on moving towards what we truly want.

Why *not* compassion?

Before exploring how to cultivate compassion in our lives, let's take a moment to address the reasons why we might *not* want to. Because despite the benefits of compassion, many of us are wary of it. We may believe that self-criticism is necessary to motivate us, and that we will become slack and lazy if we are kinder to ourselves. Or we may see compassion for ourselves as self-indulgent, self-pitying or weak. We might get hooked by stories that say we do not deserve kindness. We may fear kindness itself, if we were treated badly by caregivers when we were young, so that we came to associate kindness with mistreatment. Or we may have had little experience of kindness in our lives up to this point, and so simply not know what it means.

None of these concerns about compassion need put you off, however. Compassion is not about giving yourself permission to do nothing or to indulge in self-pity, but rather about treating yourself in a way that enables you to do what you need to. If compassion is the motivation to do what is truly best for you, then that is unlikely to involve sitting around feeling sorry for yourself. And doing what is best for you often takes courage and strength: it is not easy to face up to your difficulties and do something about them, rather than seeking to avoid them. In the case of anxiety, this will probably mean starting to accept your feelings of vulnerability and fear, rather than trying to make them go away – hardly a weak or cowardly thing to do! And finally, if you have bad memories of receiving kindness from others, or don't even know what it would be like, then we are very sorry – no one should be in that position. But if you are, then learning to be compassionate to yourself is even more important. We all need kindness and encouragement, from ourselves if not from others, and with patience and gentle effort, it is a skill that you can learn.

And if the word 'compassion' still sounds like something that you want no part of, then by all means call it something else. You might find it more appealing to work on 'being a friend to yourself', 'taking care of yourself', 'backing yourself', or anything else that works for you.

Cultivating compassion

With that said, let's begin the process of training ourselves in compassion. Because just like the other skills in this book, with regular practice, it can be learned. We can cultivate compassion in a range of ways, using words, touch, and the imagination.

Let's start with words:

Exercise 6.3
Writing a compassionate letter (Adapted from van den Brink & Coster, 2015)

Write a letter to yourself about whatever difficulties you are facing, including your anxiety, from the perspective of compassion. Try to express care for yourself, non-judgemental understanding, and a heartfelt wish to relieve your suffering. If that feels difficult, try to imagine the perspective of someone else who truly cares about you (and it's okay if you can't think of such a person – just try to imagine). And remember that it is quite alright if you do not *feel* compassionate towards yourself. The aim is to *act* compassionately towards yourself by writing this letter. So just put the words on the page.

Here are some things that you might want to include in the letter:

- *Your motivation for writing the letter*. Remind yourself that your intention is to relate to yourself with more compassion so that you can move towards a better life.

- *Acknowledgement of your suffering*. Compassion begins with recognising and opening up to suffering, rather than trying to wish it away. You might want to describe the forms your suffering takes: your thoughts and feelings, how your body feels, and how you find yourself acting. Check in with your mind and body to see how your suffering is showing up right now and reflect on how it shows up at other times.

- *Recognition that you are not alone in your suffering*. We all have our flaws and our difficulties, and all of us suffer because of them. You might want to acknowledge the reasons why you think, feel and act as you do, and that it is understandable, given your history and circumstances.

- *Kind and supportive words*, such as you might say to a friend who was suffering.

- *Encouragement*. Compassion gives us the strength to take the actions that we want to. So include some words that help you to connect with your motivation to take positive action, and the strength to do so.

For example, Carla started off by writing the following:

Carla, I am so sorry that you are suffering like this, and I want to help. You have so many worries and self-critical thoughts, and you feel so frightened and ashamed. Your throat feels so tight, and your body is so tired. You feel that you have to do everything, and so you don't let yourself rest. It must be very hard for you. Please remember that you are not alone – many other people suffer in this way. It is under-standable that things are like this for you, and you need not blame yourself: you went through a lot when you were young, and even though you have always done your best to cope, that has often meant trying to ignore your pain. That just makes things worse: you get more and more exhausted, frustrated with yourself, and miserable, and just want to give up on everything. Instead of buying into the criticism that your mind dishes out, and running around trying to do everything, why not take a break? Take a few minutes to rest, use a couple of the techniques that you have learned from The Little Anxiety Workbook, *and we can think about how you can get through this, so that you can be the mother you want to be and give your son an enjoyable day.*

Carla's letter went on to talk in more detail about some of the difficult experiences that she has had in her life, her struggles in the present, and how she can do more of the things that she cares about, all from the perspective of compassion.

When you have finished your letter, read it through, again from the perspective of compassion. Is it a truly compassionate letter, or has harshness, dismissiveness or self-criticism crept in here and there? If so, please don't let *that* become an occasion for further self-criticism. We all find it difficult to learn new ways of doing things, and compassion for ourselves is new and unfamiliar for most of us. Just use the techniques that you have already learned in this book to unhook from self-critical thoughts, open up to any pain that arises while reading your letter, and make any changes that would make your letter more compassionate.

We hope that in doing this exercise you got a sense of what it would be like to speak to yourself in a compassionate way. You don't have to write yourself a letter every time you want to do this – you can speak to yourself in the same way at any time. Whenever you are finding things difficult, see if you can connect with the same perspective from which you wrote your compassionate letter, speak to yourself in that way, and see what effect it has. You might find it helpful to keep your letter to hand, perhaps typed into your phone or recorded there as an audio file, so that you can revisit it whenever you want, as a reminder of what a compassionate perspective is like.

Now, let's try using touch as a way to express compassion for ourselves:

Exercise 6.4
Hand on heart
(Adapted from Neff, 2020)

From the very start of our lives, we are soothed by touch: babies, children and adults all want, instinctively, to be held and caressed at times of distress. Gentle touch acts directly on the nervous system to produce a sense of calmness and safety. And we don't have to wait for a good friend or family member to come along and touch us in this way – we can do it ourselves. While your mind might say that this is silly, your nervous system does not care, and learning to soothe yourself with touch can be a great way to connect with compassion in any moment.

■ When you notice that you are anxious, or under stress of any other kind, take a few breaths to ground yourself in the present moment. Follow your breath as it flows in and out, noticing the rise and fall of your chest and abdomen.

■ Now, gently place your hand over your heart, feeling the gentle pressure and warmth of your hand against your body. If you like, you can place both hands on your chest, noticing the difference between having one or both hands placed over your heart.

■ Notice the touch of your hand on your chest and the warmth flowing through it. If you want, you could gently rub your chest in a comforting gesture using small circular movements, as if you were holding a crying baby and stroking its back.

■ Notice the natural rise and fall of your chest as you breathe in and out, focusing your attention on the sense of kindness in your touch.

■ Continue for as long as you wish.

What was that like? You might have felt foolish, and your mind might have offered up criticism, perhaps both of you and of us for suggesting this exercise. But you might also have noticed a sense of safety, of being understood and cared for. So, we recommend that you unhook from any critical thoughts and practise regularly soothing yourself with touch.

And finally, let's use words, touch, and imagination all together:

Exercise 6.5
Compassion for your younger self

■ Sit comfortably, and either close your eyes or lower your gaze.

■ Tune into the sensations of breathing, and attend to them gently for a minute or two.

■ When you are ready, think of the cruellest things you some-times say to yourself, and try to remember back to when you first started to say them, or to believe that they might be true.

- Now imagine yourself at that age, as clearly as you can. Imagine your face, your hair, your clothes, and how you stood or sat.

- Picturing your younger self as clearly as you can, imagine them saying about themselves the cruel things that you say about yourself. Imagine them saying, for example, 'I'm not good at anything.' Or, 'People don't really like me.'

- Notice how you feel towards your younger self, hearing them speak about themselves in that way.

- Imagine now that you are there with your younger self. What could you say to them, that might be helpful? What wise, kind words might you offer? For example, you might say, 'I'm here for you'. Or, 'You're okay just as you are'. Imagine saying them to your younger self.

- Could you say these words to yourself now, too? Try it while placing your hand on your heart, as in the exercise above, or wherever else works for you.

- Continue with this for as long as is helpful, and then open your eyes to bring the exercise to an end.

In doing this exercise, you may have felt compassion for your younger self, and you may have been able to offer some compassionate words to them. But if you didn't feel anything, or felt something quite different, then that is okay too. Just offering kind words, whether or not you feel kind, is enough to begin to shift your relationship with your suffering.

Becoming a better teacher

Compassion is a natural part of being human: we have always cared for one another, and needed care ourselves. When we are cared for, we feel secure, and have the confidence to try new things and persist in the face of difficulties – just what we need when taking the steps needed to build the life that we want. But all too often we relate to ourselves in a harsh and critical way, which might motivate us in the short term, but over the longer term leaves us even more anxious, demoralised and likely to disengage from whatever we are doing, even if it is meaningful to us. Fortunately, we can learn to treat ourselves with greater kindness, like the kind of encouraging, supportive teacher who gets the best results, and helps us to do what we truly want to do.

Takeaways

- Remember that compassion is about relieving suffering, and means acknowledging our difficulties and relating to them with kindness.

- When we treat ourselves harshly, it is like being treated that way by someone else, and we are likely to become anxious and frantic or to disengage.

- Compassion, meanwhile, can provide us with a sense of stability and safety that enables us to try new things and persist in the face of difficulties.

- Through learning to be compassionate towards ourselves, we can move towards the life that we want.

7 Creating the life you want

Action, ultimately, is what this book is about. Without taking action, you cannot take even one step in the directions that matter to you, towards the life that you want. That life won't happen by itself: you have to actively *live* it. You have already started, of course. You have taken action by picking up this book, reading this far, and practising the skills presented here. And at the end of Chapter 5, you began to go further: you practised taking the actions that you want to, while taking painful thoughts and feelings along for the ride. In this chapter, you will go further still. We will show you how to clarify what matters most to you in life – your *values* – and how to take action in accordance with them consistently, moment by moment, as you live the life that you want.

Taking charge of your life

There is much about your life that you cannot control. You did not choose the circumstances that you were born into, or the genes that you inherited from your parents. You cannot control many of the situations that you find yourself in now. And you certainly cannot control what those around you do, or what they think and feel. You cannot even control what *you* think and feel, in any significant way. But you can control what you actually *do* and *how you do it*, and in any given moment, it can take you towards or away from the kind of life you want.

Try the following exercise to see what we mean:

Exercise 7.1
Taking control

■ Close your eyes and imagine that you have to give a presentation to a large audience. Imagine that this really matters to you. Imagine that you are at the back of the stage, ready to approach the podium, looking out at a sea of faces.

- What thoughts might be showing up? Perhaps some worries about how it is going to go, or predictions about how bad you will feel if it does not go well. Perhaps even thoughts like, 'I can't do this. I should just turn around and walk away,' or, 'They are all going to think I am ridiculous'.

- Could you stop those thoughts? Could you replace them with only happy, positive thoughts?

- Could you stop yourself feeling anxiety? Could you make yourself feel completely relaxed and at peace?

- Could you nonetheless walk towards the microphone, and begin to speak, even in the presence of these anxious thoughts and feelings?

Hopefully it is clear that, while you cannot control your thoughts and feelings (or at least not very effectively, for very long), you *can* control what you do with your arms and legs, and what you say. You may not be able to look or sound perfectly relaxed as you walk across the stage, and speak into the microphone, but you can walk and you can speak, and so you can do what matters to you in this situation. We invite you, instead of struggling with your thoughts and feelings, waiting for them to line up in such a way that you can finally be happy, to take control of the one thing that you *can* control, and start moving in the directions that matter to you.

Why wait?

We often believe that we need to feel a certain way before we can take action. We say that we will do something when we feel motivated, or when we feel less anxious. But in fact it doesn't work like that. You can act in line with what you care about no matter how you are feeling – you can approach the microphone and speak, no matter how anxious you are. If we wait to have the right feelings before we do what matters to us, we will never get off the starting blocks. Whereas if we are willing to take our anxious thoughts and feelings with us as we do what matters to us, we can begin right away. And as we explored in Chapter 5, a worthwhile life depends on doing what matters, not on having the 'right' feelings.

What to do?

This might sound all well and good, but you might be wondering what it would look like in practice. What exactly should you *do*, to move towards the life you want? The answer is that first you will have to clarify what it is that you truly want – the kind of life you want, and the person you want to be. You will have to clarify your *values*.

We are using the word 'values' in a particular way here, to mean qualities that you want to embody, simply because that is what is most meaningful and important to you. Examples of values are things like being 'courageous', 'honest' or 'spontaneous', though the list of potential values is almost endless. Whatever *you* personally care about can be a value.

When you live according to what you truly care about, life is rich and full – very different from the constricted life we lead when we try to avoid anxiety at all costs.

Let's explore in a bit more detail what values are, and how they work.

Values and goals

Values are *qualities* that you can bring to your actions. This makes them different from goals. A goal is a destination that you aim at, whereas a value is more like a direction that you want to go in. It's like the difference between heading for California and heading West. This is important because it means that:

- *You can always act in line with your values.* Once you have achieved a goal, such as reaching California, then it is not clear what you should do next. Whereas you can *always* find a way to be 'kind' or 'honest', just as you can always keep on heading West.

- *You cannot fail.* If you do not achieve a goal, then you have failed and, again, it may not be clear what comes next. Whereas if you are not courageous or honest in one moment, you can always be so in the next, perhaps in a new way.

- *There is always a way to act in line with values.* Goals are quite specific – either you do what you had planned to, or you do not. Whereas values can be expressed in a wide range of ways. For example, you may not have been courageous in confronting your boss, but you can still be courageous in speaking up in a meeting.

- *Values are always in the present moment.* Goals generally lie in the future or the past. Either we are thinking about how to achieve them, or we are looking back at our successes or failures. Whereas values are right here, right now. When we orient ourselves towards our values, we focus on living them out in *this* moment, and *this* one. We can experience immediately the sense of vitality that comes with acting in line with our values, which just might motivate us to keep on doing so.

None of which is to say that goals are bad. Rather, they are a crucial part of the journey through life. But in a life lived according to values, goals are staging posts along the way, that help to structure the journey, rather than the point of the journey. So, if we value 'Courage', we might set a goal of giving a presentation at the annual staff meeting. But that is not an endpoint. After we have done that (and before it, as well), we can live out the value of courage in all kinds of other ways. With values as our guide, life becomes a journey filled with meaning and satisfaction. Whereas if we take goals as our lodestar, we fixate on our destination and fail to appreciate the journey.

Values are personal

Values are what *you* value, deep in your heart, not what you think you *should* value. Often, if asked what we value, we will talk about qualities that we have been taught are 'good', or that are valued in the wider culture. Of course, you *could* truly value those qualities, deep in your heart, and indeed many of us will find that we share values such as honesty, connection with others and fairness. But equally you may not – there are no *right* or *wrong* values.

Values are not rules

As discussed above, our values cannot be dictated to us by others. They also cannot be dictated to us by rules that our minds set for us, or by our need to avoid certain feelings. Often, what at first appears to be a value – something that inspires and uplifts us – turns out to be a rule that our mind has laid down. For example, we might say that we value kindness, but in fact we are following a rule that says, 'I *should* be kind to everyone'. And often we follow rules because we are unwilling to feel certain feelings. Perhaps when we break our rule about kindness, we feel guilty, or perhaps our mind created the rule in the first place because we fear that if we do not always make others happy, they might reject us. In either case, our commitment to kindness arises not because it is something that we truly want to move *towards*, but rather because it enables us to stay *away* from guilt, anxiety and the pain of rejection. Values are freely chosen, in that our pursuit of them does not have this quality of rigidity and compulsion. We pursue them because we want to, not because we have to. And when we do so, we might notice a sense of freedom and ease, rather than the tension and agitation that comes with taking action because we are compelled to, in order to escape our own painful feelings or self-criticism.

Values are best held lightly

If our values are a matter of preference rather than compulsion, then we will pursue them wholeheartedly but hold them lightly. We will not feel that we *should* or *must* hold to them, and we will be able to revise them or put them aside when that is the most workable thing to do. Sometimes it may not be workable to pursue a value in a particular context. 'Kindness' may take a back seat to 'honesty', for example, when there is a painful truth that someone in your life needs to hear. And it is quite natural to change your values over time – they will evolve as you and your life do. Values are only as good as the contribution that they make, in any given moment, to a life well-lived.

What are your values?

In order to live by our values, we first have to work out what they are. This will need some careful reflection – as we have said above, what you at first think are your values might turn out to be rules that you have picked up from others, or efforts to avoid pain, including anxiety. Or you may simply have no idea what your values are. If your life has become focused on avoiding anxiety, you may have lost touch with your deeper desires. You may not know what you would want to do if you gave up the struggle with anxiety.

This realisation can be painful, and could make you want to put down this book and forget about clarifying and living by your values. You may be tempted to retreat back into avoidance. If so, we hope that you will be able to make good use of the skills you have learned so far. Stay connected with the here-and-now, rather than disappearing into anxious problem-solving. Unhook from your negative or anxious thoughts. Open up to your painful feelings. And above all, be kind to yourself.

Before we get to work on clarifying your values, a few points that will help with the process:

- You can have different values in different areas of your life. For example, you might value closeness in your family relationships, but professionalism at work. So you will need to apply the exercises presented below to more than one area of your life.

■ Sometimes values can conflict, in which case you will need to decide which is most relevant and important in the situation at hand. For instance, if you value both kindness and independence in your relationships, you may sometimes have to choose between them. You can think of your values as like the countries on a spinning globe. As the globe spins, some countries come to the fore, while others are hidden. But it won't be long before those that are hidden come into view once more.

■ Values can change over time, so there is no need to worry about getting it perfectly 'right' at this stage. Repeat the exercises below from time to time, to refine and update your values, as your circumstances change.

So, with all that said, let's start to clarify your values:

Exercise 7.2
Pick your values
(Adapted from Harris, 2008)

The most straightforward way to start homing in on your values is to pick from a list, such as the one below (which is hardly exhaustive – you can search online to find many more lists with many more values). Read through the values listed and sort them into 'very important', 'important', and 'somewhat important', or simply pick out the five that seem most important to you.

1. *Adventure*: to be adventurous; to actively explore novel or stimulating experiences

2. *Assertiveness*: to respectfully stand up for my rights and request what I want

3. *Authenticity*: to be authentic, genuine and real; to be true to myself

4. *Connection*: to engage fully in whatever I'm doing and be fully present with others

5. *Courage*: to be courageous or brave; to persist in the face of fear, threat or difficulty

6. *Creativity*: to be creative or innovative

7. *Curiosity*: to be curious, open-minded and interested; to explore and discover

8. *Fairness and justice*: to be fair and just to myself or others

9. *Flexibility*: to adjust and adapt readily to changing circumstances

10. *Freedom and independence*: to choose how I live and help others do likewise

11. *Friendliness*: to be friendly, companionable or agreeable towards others

12. *Gratitude*: to be grateful for and appreciative of myself, others and life

13. *Honesty*: to be honest, truthful and sincere with myself and others

14. *Industry*: to be industrious, hardworking and dedicated

15. *Intimacy*: to open up, reveal and share myself, emotionally or physically

16. *Kindness*: to be kind, considerate, nurturing or caring towards myself or others

17. *Order*: to be orderly and organised

18. *Persistence and commitment*: to continue resolutely, despite problems or difficulties

19. *Respect/self-respect*: to treat myself and others with care and consideration

20. *Trust*: to be trustworthy; to be loyal, faithful, sincere and reliable

Hopefully you are starting to get a sense of your values. We would encourage you not to stop there, though, but rather to try out the other exercises that follow. Picking values from a list is a great way to get a feel for them, but it is inevitably somewhat prescriptive. To really connect with *your* values, try some of the other approaches that we suggest.

Follow your fulfilment

Certain moments in our lives feel particularly fulfilling and meaningful, and that can be a sign that we are in contact with one or more of our values. So, at such times, you can stop and ask yourself:

What is it that feels so meaningful in this situation? What qualities does it have that are bringing me fulfilment? What qualities am I expressing that are important to me?

The answers may point you towards a value that you hold but are not aware of.

But you don't have to wait until you next feel especially fulfilled to use this method of clarifying values. Just try the following exercise:

Exercise 7.3
The sweet spot

■ Sit comfortably and either close your eyes or lower your gaze.

- Tune into the sensations of breathing and attend to them gently for a minute or two.

- Think back to a time that was particularly good for you, in a way that seemed meaningful and deeply satisfying. It might have lasted just a few moments, or it might have lasted weeks or months.

- Connect with it in your memory as vividly as you can – the sights, the sounds and the feelings. Now, ask yourself what qualities made this time so meaningful. They could be qualities of the situation, or qualities that you showed in the situation. Those might be some of your values.

- When you are ready, open your eyes to bring the exercise to an end.

You can, of course, use this method 'on the go' as well. Whenever you notice yourself experiencing a sense of meaning and vitality, really engaging with and finding satisfaction in the present moment, ask yourself what makes it so sweet. See if you can connect with what you are valuing in that moment. This should become easier as you continue to practise the skills in Chapter 2. With greater awareness of the present moment, it becomes easier to notice moments of fulfilment, satisfaction and meaning, and to discover what truly matters to you.

What hurts, matters

As we said at the beginning of the chapter, finding a situation painful can mean that it *matters* to you – behind the pain might be hiding a value! Use the following exercise to peer behind your pain and catch a glimpse of your values.

Exercise 7.4
Look behind your pain

- Think of an issue that really bothers you, in your own life or in the wider world.

- Take a few moments to get in touch with your sense of unhappiness about it.

- Now ask yourself:
  o What is it that I care about here that leads me to feel upset?
  o What, in other words, would I have to *not* care about in order to *not* be upset by this situation? Perhaps that thing that you care about is a value!

Again, you can also use this method on the go. When you notice yourself feeling upset or anxious, it is worth asking yourself whether a value is in play, and what it might be. You might find that this painful experience is in fact valuable, because it reveals a value! For example, in Chapter 5, Amir felt painful anxiety as he prepared to meet his girlfriend's friends. Had he reflected that pain and values are two sides of the same coin, and asked what was on the other side, he might have realised that he felt anxious because he had an opportunity to do something that truly mattered to him: to strengthen his connection with his girlfriend.

Looking back

Values are what you most want your life to be about; the qualities that you most want to embody and the things that you want to stand for. But they can be hard to remember, or even to be aware of in the first place, especially in the midst of anxiety. Which means that it can help, when reflecting on them, to take up the perspective of yourself ten years from now, looking back. Let's try it.

Exercise 7.5

Looking back ten years from now
(Adapted from Harris, 2019)

- Sit comfortably, and either close your eyes or lower your gaze.

- Tune into the sensations of breathing, and for a few moments follow them as best you can.

- Now, imagine that you are in the future, ten years from now. You are looking back on your life as it is today.

- Complete the following statements:
  - o 'I did not spend enough time doing things like. . .'
  - o 'If I could travel back in time, what I would do differently is. . .'

- When you are ready to bring the exercise to a close, return your attention to your breath for a moment, and then lift your gaze or open your eyes.

- Write down your answers to the questions above.

- Perhaps your answers reveal what you truly care about. What values can you identify, based on your answers to these questions? Write them down.

Your answers to these questions are likely to highlight some of
your values: the qualities that you want to embody and live by.
They reveal how·you *truly* want to spend your time, what you want
to stand for in life, and what you want to focus on.

Aligning with values

Clarifying values is, of course, not the end of the story. Once we
know what our values are, we need to live by them. This will mean
considering how fully we are already living by our values, and then
planning to do so more fully. We will need to work out what we
want to do, and then we will need to. . . do it.

In a moment, we will have a look at how far you are already living
in accordance with your values. But please remember the skills
that you have been learning – none of us live by our values as fully
as we would like, and it can be painful to see clearly the distance
between where we are and where we would like to be. We hope
that, as you reflect on the distance between you and your values,
you will be able to stay connected to the present moment, unhook
from any self-critical thoughts, open up to any pain that you feel,
and, most of all, be kind to yourself as you explore your current
relationship to your values.

Exercise 7.6

Take a closer look at your life
(Adapted from Wilson, Sandoz, Kitchens, & Roberts, 2010)

For each of the areas of your life listed in the table below, see if
you can come up with at least one value – perhaps drawing upon
those that you have already identified in the preceding exercises.

Area of life	Values
Relationships and family	E.g. being supportive; being patient
Work and education	E.g. being diligent; being ambitious
Recreation and health	E.g. being adventurous; being physically active

■ Now, if you like, think about which other areas of your life you
would like to identify values for.

■ You might break up the areas listed above into smaller sub-
areas. For example, 'relationships and family' could be broken
up into 'intimate relationship/marriage', 'birth family', 'parent-
ing' and 'friends'.

■ Or you might come up with completely new areas. For
example, 'community engagement' or 'spirituality'.

■ For each of these areas, come up with at least one value.

You should now have a fairly comprehensive set of values; enough to start moving your life in the direction that you want to go. Now, let's see how much you are living by these values already, and in which areas of your life there is the most room for improvement. And if there seems a be a lot of room for improvement, then that need not be an occasion for despair, anxiety or self-criticism. It just means that you have a big opportunity in front of you.

Exercise 7.7
Take stock of your values
(Adapted from Wilson et al., 2010)

For each of the areas of life that you have considered above, ask yourself:

- How important is this area of my life to me? Give the answer as a score of 1–10, where 1 is 'completely unimportant' and 10 is 'very important'.

- How much have I managed to live by my value(s) in this area of life, during the past week? Give the answer as a score of 1–10, where 1 is 'not at all', and 10 is 'totally'.

In doing this exercise, you should start to see where you can most usefully focus your efforts to live by your values. You might want to focus on those areas that score highly for 'importance' but not so highly for 'living by my values', as it is here that the greatest gains can be made. And once again, please don't let this become an occasion for self-criticism or despair (and if self-criticism does arise, there is no need to become self-critical about *that*). We all struggle to live in line with our values, and in order to move closer to them we will sometimes need to see how we are doing, feel any pain that comes with doing so, and start planning to change things.

But before we start to make a plan, let's see how Nicole, who we met in Chapters 1 and 4, got on with clarifying her values.

Nicole has had enough of being controlled by her anxiety. She has been doing the exercises from *The Little Anxiety Workbook*, and she can see more clearly what has been happening. She can see where she has been going wrong, but she doesn't really know what she should do instead – she has been so busy for so long with trying to keep her anxiety at bay that she can't even remember what she *wants* anymore. It's hopeless, she thinks, but she knows that that is just her mind talking; and so she thanks it for its input and resolves to take a proper look at how things stand, no matter how painful that might be.

First, she does a few minutes of Mindful Breathing, to connect with the present moment. And then she asks herself, 'Just what am I so upset about? What would I have to *not* care about in order to not get so anxious about work?' She takes care to connect with her body as she asks this question. The answer, if there is one, needs to come from her heart and her guts, not just her head. 'Doing my best,' comes the answer, and she writes it down on the piece of paper she has set out in front of her. She just wants to do her best, but her mind gets involved and tells her that if she hasn't worked herself half to death, and if her work isn't perfect, then she can't have done her best. And obeying the rules set for her by her mind is not helping her to do her best – it's actually holding her back at work and in other areas of her life. She turns the value of 'doing my best' over in her mind, feeling that, yes, that's probably it.

Next, she searches her memory for a time in her life that felt particularly joyous and fulfilling. She doesn't have to search for long: she often thinks back to her holiday after graduation with a few friends from university. It might be the very best time she can remember. She felt so free, so connected to the present moment, and so connected to her friends. It was glorious. Perhaps those are some of her values, she thinks, and writes down 'freedom', 'being in the present moment', and 'connection with others'. She certainly hasn't been able to pursue those values much lately, while trying to keep her anxiety at bay. But she can start to, she thinks, and reads on to the next section of *The Little Anxiety Workbook*.

Making a plan

However far you might be from your values, it is within your power to take action and do things differently. So let's start to think about how, in practical terms, you can move towards your values by identifying and pursuing appropriate goals. But first, some tips on what kind of goals and plans are likely to be most helpful.

Start small

There are many actions that you can take to move towards any given value, and it is best to start with small, manageable ones. There is no point in setting yourself a big goal that you cannot achieve, when instead you could start small, build your confidence, and move on to the bigger goals further down the line. You can even take a bigger goal and break it down into a series of smaller steps. That way you can start right away, but without feeling like you are climbing a mountain. When climbing Everest, it is probably better to focus just on getting to Base Camp first, rather than having your eyes glued to the (seemingly) unreachable summit.

As you begin your journey, you just might start to discover the sense of vitality that comes from acting in accordance with your values. And this will provide you with the motivation for your next step, and your next. Bit by bit, through pursuing your values in each moment, more and more of your life can be brought into line with them.

Be clear

It is much easier to pursue a clear, well-defined goal than a vague one. That way, you will know just what you have to do, and when (or whether) you have done it. A popular way of developing such goals is to make them SMART. This means that they should be:

- **S**pecific. Be clear about the actions that you will take. For example, replace vague goals like, 'I will not over-prepare for meetings at work', with specific ones, such as, 'I will spend no more than one hour preparing for each meeting at work'. To be even more specific, ask yourself questions such as, 'What do I want to achieve?' 'Who is involved?' 'Where will it happen?' and, 'When will it happen?'

- **M**easurable. How will you know when you have accomplished this goal? In the example above, it is very easy to know whether or not you spent more than an hour preparing for a meeting. It would be harder to decide whether you 'over-prepared' for a meeting.

- **A**daptive. The point of pursuing goals is to live more in line with values. But it is easy to forget that, and so it is important to keep your values in mind when developing your goals, and ask yourself, 'Does this goal map directly onto one of my values?'

- **R**ealistic. There is no point in setting yourself goals that you cannot achieve – you will get nowhere and will become demoralised. For instance, becoming a national triathlon champion may be beyond you, and so a more modest goal, such as exercising three times per week, would be more helpful. In order to decide whether your goal is realistic, you can ask yourself whether you have the necessary resources to achieve it. For example, the time, money, facilities, physical health, social support, knowledge and skills. Does anything need to be put in place before it can be done? If so, then getting those resources together might be a suitable goal for you to pursue first.

■ **T**ime-bound. Without a time limit, you may never get round to achieving your goal. So, give it a time limit, and perhaps also specify when you will take the particular actions that are needed to achieve your goal.

With all of that said, let's have a go at developing some goals to move you closer to your values and the life that you want.

Exercise 7.8
Plan your next move

Pick one of the values that you identified in Exercise 7.7 as being very important to you, but which you are not managing to remain very faithful to. Think about what actions you can take over the short and longer term in line with that value. Your actions don't have to be building up to a significant goal. Sometimes they might do, but it is also fine for smaller actions to stand on their own. But remember to make each goal a SMART goal.

Fill in a table like the one below, which Nicole filled in for her value of 'freedom'.

	What I can do to live in accordance with my value in the next. . .				
Value	Year	Month	Week	Day	Hour
Freedom	Go travelling	Set aside a Sunday to make no plans and do whatever I feel like	Go for a mindful walk at lunchtime instead of working	Do some research on places I could go travelling	Stop working for a minute and have a cup of tea

Once you have done this for one of your values, try it with a couple of others.

Taking action

So now you have a plan, and the only thing left is to actually . . . do it. Of course, this is where we often come undone. All of us have had the experience of making plans and failing to follow through on them. Here are some tips to give you the best possible chance of achieving your value-based goals.

Share your intentions

We are more likely to follow through on our plans when we have committed to them publicly, thus making ourselves accountable for them. To do this, simply tell a friend or family member what you intend to do, and perhaps check in with them regularly as you take steps towards your goals.

Prepare for hitches

Few things that are worth doing go completely smoothly, and so, as you take committed action in line with your values, you are almost certain to encounter difficulties. These might be external – practical obstacles to your pursuit of your goals – or they might be internal – thoughts and feelings that make you want to retreat back to your usual way of doing things. And watch out for internal obstacles masquerading as external ones: when your mind makes up spurious reasons why you can't do things that make you feel anxious. It is well worth thinking about all of these obstacles in advance, and planning how you will stay on track.

Let's try to identify, and plan to meet, some of these obstacles. Fill in a table like the one below, which we have filled in with an example from Nicole.

Exercise 7.9
Be prepared

What is my value-based goal?	What thoughts might get in my way?	What feelings might get in my way?	What external obstacles might get in my way?	What can I do to meet these challenges?
e.g. go travelling	'I won't be fulfilling my potential at work' 'People will think I am not serious about work'	Fear Guilt	Money	Use the skills I have learned to unhook from thoughts (Chapter 3) and open up to my feelings (Chapter 5); remember that 'fulfilling my potential' does not just mean fulfilling it at work — it means living a full life in accordance with my values; start putting aside money each month

Remember your values

When you encounter difficult feelings and thoughts on the road towards the life you want, remember why you are doing what you are doing – keep your values front and centre in your mind. It is much easier to be willing to experience pain when you know that it is part of the life that you want to live. You could write your values down on your phone and refer to them whenever things get difficult, or take a few moments to reflect on them when you wake up in the morning

Encourage yourself and be kind

As discussed in Chapter 6, it is tough being human at the best of times, and we do better in facing the challenges of life when we encourage ourselves kindly rather than criticising ourselves harshly. With compassion for yourself, you will be better able to keep going, in the direction of your values, when difficulties and setbacks show up.

Losing your way

There will inevitably be times when you drift away from your values, or even forget about them altogether. Over and over again, you might find that your anxiety has taken control of you, and that you are following its commands instead of acting in line with your values. This is completely normal, and no occasion for shame, hopelessness or self-criticism. We all get pulled away from our values every single day and it is a great opportunity to practise all the skills set out in this book. When you notice that it has happened, simply reconnect with your values and adjust your behaviour accordingly. The commitment to living a value-driven life is a commitment to noticing, over and over again, when we have drifted off track, and recommitting ourselves to the path of value-led action.

And finally, when it comes to valued action, there really is no time like the present: you can start right now. So, take a moment to think of something you could do *right now* to move in the direction of one of your values, by even a tiny bit. And, having thought of it, would you be willing to do it? If so, put down this book, and begin your journey towards the life that you want, right now.

Ready for action

None of our good intentions can bear fruit without action. But to act on those intentions, we first need to know what they are. We need to clarify what it is that really matters to us in life. We need to clarify our *values*.

Values are the directions that we want to move in, simply because they are what we *value*, rather than because of what others expect of us, or because we are determined not to feel bad. When we act in line with our values, our lives can be meaningful, satisfying and vital. Values are distinct from goals, which are fixed points that we aim at; rather, they are qualities of action that we can embody in any moment. Unlike goals, you can never get to the end of your values.

Once we have clarified our values (or even one value!) it is time to act. And here goals can serve values: to move in the directions that we want to go, we will need fixed points to aim at along the way. We will need goals that are small (to start with) and SMART, and we will need to be ready for all of the challenges that might show up as we pursue them. As well as making use of all the skills covered in previous chapters, we will need to keep our values firmly in mind as we seek to live in accordance to them, and remember that anxiety is often a sign that we are going in the right direction, rather than a reason to stop. And when we find ourselves pulled off track, we can simply recommit to our values and take action in line with them in the very next moment.

Takeaways

■ Remember that action is the most important part of breaking free from anxiety.

■ To take action, you will need to clarify your values: the directions that you want to move in. Values are different from goals, are personal, and are freely chosen.

■ You will need to set goals that serve your values. They should be small (to start with) and SMART.

■ In pursuing your goals, you will need to prepare for challenges, keep your values in mind, and recommit to them whenever you find yourself pulled off track.

■ And please remember, in every moment, to treat yourself with compassion.

8 The beginning

This is the last chapter of *The Little Anxiety Workbook*, so congratulations! You have now learned all of the skills that you need to reclaim your life from anxiety. But your job is not done – in fact it is just beginning – because now you have to actually *use* those skills. In order to move towards the life that you want, you will need to practise them regularly, so that they come more and more naturally, and you will need to deploy them at the moments when anxiety threatens to take control. In this final chapter, we will give you tools to help you do this.

A seamless whole

When you are stuck, struggling with anxiety, you act rigidly, doing the same old things, even though they aren't working. In order to free yourself from the grip of anxiety, meanwhile, you will need to act *flexibly*: to respond appropriately to the demands of the moment. And the next one. And the next.

We have laid out four distinct processes that keep you trapped in anxiety, and several skills that you can use to develop flexibility. Note that we make no promise that you will get rid of the processes that are causing your difficulties. That would not be possible – because human beings do not have a 'delete' function – and nor would it be desirable, because these processes might be useful under some circumstances. In order to write this book, for example, we have had to lose touch with the here-and-now and get thoroughly immersed in our thoughts. And so, instead of seeking to rid yourself of the processes that are causing you trouble, we suggest that with the new skills that you have learned, you can meet each moment with a workable response, and move forwards in the directions that matter to you.

Let's remind ourselves of the four processes, and the skills that we can use to meet them.

Four processes that maintain anxiety	Skills to loosen the grip of anxiety and get back on track
Losing awareness	Present-moment awareness and flexible attention
Getting hooked	Unhooking from thoughts Being more than the story Willingness to have feelings
Being harsh and critical	Compassion
Not doing what matters	Knowing what matters Doing what matters

. . . all of which you can remember, of course, using the handy acronym **FREE**, which you learned in Chapter 1:

F - ocus on what is right here, right now;

R - elease your struggle with thoughts and feelings;

E - ncourage yourself with a kindly attitude; and

E - ngage in the actions that matter to you.

In fact, neither the processes nor the skills are really distinct. All of the four processes knit together and reinforce each other, so that anxiety, when you are in the grip of it, feels like a knot that you cannot unpick. And your new skills knit together into a whole that you can use fluidly to meet the demands of the moment.

When you first begin to use your new skills, it might feel a bit awkward, and you might have to think about what you are doing. Recall, for example, the analogy of learning to play a musical instrument. At first, it will take effort and conscious intention to make your fingers do what they need to, and to read the music in front of you. But over time, these skills will become smooth and instinctive, and weave together into a fluid whole. It can be like that with the skills that we have presented in this book. With practice, you will know intuitively what is needed in any given moment, and know from your own experience how the skills overlap and support one another.

Let's see what this looks like in practice:

Amir is determined that this time he is going to go through with it. After the last time, when he bailed out of meeting Zeina's friends, things were not so good between them. It was very clear to him how his behaviour had affected things. Much clearer than it usually would have been, as he has been practising techniques for noticing what is going on right here, right now, rather than spending so much time lost in his thoughts (*Present-moment awareness and flexible attention*). He reflected on the whole situation, and saw clearly that what matters to him in this situation is strengthening his connection with Zeina (*Knowing what matters*). He worked out how he could do it – by attending the party that they are going to tonight (*Doing what matters*) – and resolved to go through with it no matter what thoughts or feelings show up (*Unhooking from thoughts; Willingness to have feelings*).

Now that they are on their way, he notices the usual obstacles showing up (*Present-moment awareness and flexible attention*): worries about what will go wrong, tightness in his throat and an urge to turn and run, and his 'I'm so pathetic' story playing on repeat in his mind. But he remembers the acronym **FREE**, and knows what to do. He keeps his attention on the sensations of his body, noticing with curiosity how his anxiety is showing up there (*Willingness to have feelings*). From time to time, he reminds himself, 'I'm having the thought that. . .' (*Unhooking from thoughts*). And most important, he remembers why he is doing this (*Knowing what matters*) and just keeps on heading towards the party (*Doing what matters*), no matter what his mind says to him, or how powerful his urge to run away (*Unhooking from thoughts; Willingness to have feelings*).

They arrive at the bar where the party is being held, and his anxiety goes up another notch. He is scared to go in, and he is scared that Zeina will see how scared he is and think that he is pathetic. But that's just his mind's story about him, he reminds himself (*Unhooking from thoughts*), and pats his phone in his pocket, where he has written down this story to remind himself that it is just that – a story – and need not control him (*Being more than the story*). He tries out a more compassionate perspective: that everyone gets anxious, and that it's natural for it to happen in the situations that we care about (*Compassion; Knowing what matters*). He resolves to be kind to himself, whatever the outcome of the evening (*Compassion*). Feeling a little more resilient, and willing to feel his anxiety as he faces whatever challenges await him at the party, he takes Zeina's hand and crosses the threshold (*Willingness to have feelings; Doing what matters*).

Amir has been practising the skills from *The Little Anxiety Workbook*, and so he is able to see clearly how his habitual patterns of behaviour are affecting him, to see clearly how he *truly* wants to behave, and then to do it, despite all of the anxious thoughts and feelings that try to get in his way. He is able to respond flexibly to the situation that he is in. And with practise, you can do the same.

A new perspective: the Matrix

We will now introduce you to the Matrix (Adapted from Polk, Schoendorff, Webster, & Olaz, 2016), which is a tool that pulls together everything that you have learned in this book, and can help you to apply it. Let's take a look at it.

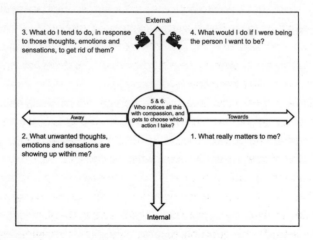

In any situation, the Matrix can help you to map out what you are experiencing, notice what is driving your behaviour, unhook from any difficult thoughts, emotions and sensations, and decide what to do next. It takes you through these six questions:

1. *What really matters to me? (Bottom right quadrant)*
   Here you identify your values: what is it that you really care
   about in this situation?

2. *What unwanted thoughts, emotions and sensations are showing up*
   within me? (Bottom left quadrant)
   This is an invitation to notice what thoughts, emotions and
   sensations make this situation challenging for you.

3. *What do I tend to do in response to those thoughts, emotions and sensa-*
   tions, to get rid of them? (Top left quadrant)
   Here you identify your 'away moves': the behaviours, usually habitual
   ones, that you use to escape from the painful thoughts, emotions and
   sensations that you identified in the bottom left quadrant.
     Note that these behaviours should be ones that someone else
   could see you doing, such as 'leaving the party and going home',
   rather than things that you do internally, such as 'worrying' or
   'trying to think of things to say'. There is a picture of a video
   camera with this question, to remind you of this. Imagine filming
   yourself in this situation and then watching the film afterwards,
   to see your 'away moves'.
     And if you do things internally to get away from your painful
   thoughts and feelings, then write down what someone else could see

you doing at around that time (or what you could see, watching your-self later on film). For example, while you are 'worrying', you could be seen disengaging from conversations and staring into space, and as a result of your worrying, you could be seen leaving the party.

4. *What would I do if I were being the person I want to be? (Top right quadrant)*
Here you identify possible 'towards moves': actions that will take you in the direction of your values. Again, these should be things that someone else could see you doing. For example, 'Starting a conversation with someone new at the party', rather than, 'Telling myself to start a conversation'. Again, there is a video camera with this question, to remind you of this. If you filmed yourself moving in the direction of your values in this situation, what would you see when you watched the film afterward?

5. *Who is noticing all this? And who gets to choose whether you move away from painful thoughts, emotions and sensations or towards what matters? (Central circle)*
With this question, you connect with the perspective of aware-ness, and realise that *that* is who you truly are, rather than the story that your mind likes to tell about you.

6. *Can I be compassionate as I notice all this? (Central circle)*
   And finally, with this question you connect with the compassion that makes it easier to do what matters to you.

In the Matrix, these questions are set out spatially, so that you can see more clearly how they all fit together. The boxes in the lower half of the Matrix represent things that exist within you, that no one else could see (i.e. your thoughts and feelings), whereas those in the top half represent the things that others could see you do. And in the middle is the awareness (i.e. you) that notices all of this, that chooses how to respond, and that views it all with compassion.

Confronted with a challenging situation, the awareness at the centre of the Matrix (the awareness that is *you*) can see clearly that if you want to experience the contents of the bottom right quadrant (the things that you care about), you will need to *do* the contents of the top right quadrant (the actions that take you towards what you care about). This will often mean refraining from doing the contents of the top left quadrant (the actions that take you away from painful thoughts and feelings), which in turn means that you will need to be willing to have the contents of the bottom left quadrant (the unwanted thoughts, emotions and sensations that show up in this situation).

Whenever you run into a challenging situation, you can call the Matrix to mind, ask yourself the six questions within it, and see which actions will take you in the directions that you really want to go. Here is an example that Amir filled in to describe his experience in the case example above.

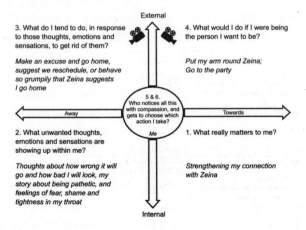

External

3. What do I tend to do, in response to those thoughts, emotions and sensations, to get rid of them?

Make an excuse and go home, suggest we reschedule, or behave so grumpily that Zeina suggests I go home

4. What would I do if I were being the person I want to be?

Put my arm round Zeina; Go to the party

5 & 6.
Who notices all this with compassion, and gets to choose which action I take?

Away ← → **Towards**

Me

2. What unwanted thoughts, emotions and sensations are showing up within me?

Thoughts about how wrong it will go and how bad I will look, my story about being pathetic, and feelings of fear, shame and tightness in my throat

1. What really matters to me?

Strengthening my connection with Zeina

Internal

Now, we'd like you to practise by filling in a Matrix for yourself.

Exercise 8.1

Mapping out your anxiety

Think of an anxiety-provoking situation that comes up fairly often for you. For instance, it might be attending social gatherings, or speaking up in meetings at work. Now, for this situation, fill in each of the four quadrants of the Matrix and its centre, using your answers to the six questions set out there. You can draw out a Matrix of your own, like the one below.

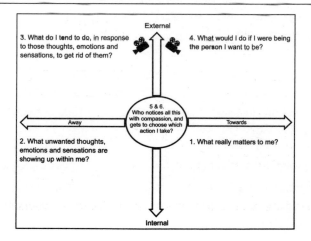

External

3. What do I tend to do, in response to those thoughts, emotions and sensations, to get rid of them?

4. What would I do if I were being the person I want to be?

Away

5 & 6.
Who notices all this with compassion, and gets to choose which action I take?

Towards

2. What unwanted thoughts, emotions and sensations are showing up within me?

1. What really matters to me?

Internal

Once you have filled out your Matrix, take a look at the left side. Notice how it contains all the old, habitual stuff: the anxious thoughts, emotions and sensations that you want to get rid of (bottom left quadrant), and the actions that you take in order to make them go away (top left quadrant). Maybe some of this is the same as what you wrote down in Exercise 1.1, back in Chapter 1. And maybe you can notice that your efforts to get rid of your thoughts and feelings are ineffective and take you away from the life that you want. Over the short term, you might experience relief from your anxiety, but it always comes back, often more intensely, and over the longer term, your life shrinks and is drained of meaning. Amir, for example, fears rejection and disconnection from others (bottom left quadrant), and so he tries to reduce his anxiety by keeping his distance from them (top left quadrant). But in doing so, he increases his sense of disconnection (bottom left quadrant), risks rejection by his girlfriend, and moves further away from what he most wants: to connect with her (bottom right quadrant).

Now take a look at the right side of your Matrix. Here are your values (bottom right quadrant), and the actions that you can take that would be in line with them (top right quadrant). Reflect on how your life might change if you acted consistently in that way.

For Amir, it means going to the party with his girlfriend in order to strengthen the connection between them.

And finally, notice who is noticing all this: awareness itself, which is *you* (central circle). And see if you can connect with some sense of compassion for yourself, here in this situation, experiencing all of this, and bring some compassion to your efforts to take the actions that you care about. You might find it helpful to place a hand on your heart or to say some kind words to yourself, or use any other techniques from Chapter 6 that work for you.

To help you to work your way around the Matrix and apply it in your life, you might find it useful to ask yourself the questions in the following exercise:

Exercise 8.2
Acting on the Matrix

1. *Have the actions (in the top left quadrant) that I have taken to deal with my unwanted thoughts, emotions and sensations helped me:*

a. *To get rid of those unwanted thoughts, emotions and sensations in the short term?*
(The answer is usually 'Yes')
b. *To get rid of those unwanted thoughts, emotions and sensations in the long term?*
(The answer is usually 'No')
c. *To move any closer towards who and what really matters to me?*
(The answer is usually 'No')

2. *In order to never again experience my unwanted thoughts, emotions and sensations (in the bottom left quadrant), what would I have to give up on and not care about (in the bottom right quadrant)?*

3. *If my painful thoughts and feelings (in the bottom left quadrant) were connected to those things that matter to me (in the bottom right quadrant), would I choose to make room for them so that I could have those things that are important to me?*

And if the answer to that final question is 'Yes', then perhaps it is time to take action, in the direction of what truly matters to you!

Practising the Matrix

Of course, like everything else in this book, the Matrix will not be much use to you unless you practise using it, and so we recommend that you draw out and complete a Matrix at least three times this week, in relation to any challenging situations that you experience. They need not be the most challenging situations that you encounter – any challenge will do, no matter how small. The idea is to practise using the Matrix as much as possible, so that using it becomes a habit.

You can use the Matrix to map out either situations that you have already experienced, or ones that you know are coming up. And when you are actually in challenging situations, see if you can use the six questions from the Matrix to guide your behaviour. At first it might be difficult to remember the questions or see how they fit together, but with practise you will probably start to 'see' the Matrix in your mind, and using it can become as easy and intuitive as any of your existing habits.

Getting back on track

Although you are now equipped with powerful tools to help you reclaim your life from anxiety, it will not all be plain sailing from here.

Your anxious thoughts and feelings will of course not disappear – and nor do they need to. They will continue to show up, but they need not trap you and pull you away from the life that you want – if you use your new skills. But there may also be times when your old habits start to reassert themselves, and you find yourself acting out the same old patterns of behaviour, that lead you away from the life that you want and towards one dominated by anxiety. This might happen because of your circumstances. You might find yourself going through an unusually stressful time, and the intensity and frequency of your anxious thoughts and feelings might increase and begin to take control of you. Or you might find yourself making less use of the techniques that you have learned in this book, perhaps even because things have been going particularly well for you. Either way, this is natural and to be expected. We all get pulled away from our values, and we all slip back into old, habitual behaviour patterns. So please don't be hard on yourself if it happens to you. The solution is to simply re-engage with the newer, more helpful habits that you have been building while reading this book.

One way to do this is to use the Matrix. As well as using it for particular situations that you find yourself in, you can use it to look at how things are going for you more generally in your life. You can note: the main values that are important to you in life, the thoughts and feelings that you find challenging, the behaviours that you use to try to get rid of those thoughts and feelings, and the behaviours that you think would be more helpful.

And to make a more detailed plan to get back on track, we recommend that you:

- Take some time to read again about values, in Chapter 7. Remind yourself of what it is that you truly care about and reflect on how close you are to it at the moment.

- Again using Chapter 7, set goals that will move you towards your values and away from a life of struggling with your anxiety. Set SMART goals for the next day, week and month.

- Think about which exercises from this book you can use along the way to respond to any internal obstacles (i.e. thoughts and feelings) that might otherwise pull you off track. You might decide to practise some exercises more regularly than you have been, and to use particular exercises in particular situations.

- Anticipate any external obstacles that might get in your way, and think about practical ways to deal with them.

- And, once again, be kind to yourself (see Chapter 6) – remember that it is very common for there to be ups as well as downs on the road to a better life.

To help you think through these steps and get back on track, fill in a table like this. We have filled it in with an example from Carla, who we met in Chapters 3 and 6.

Exercise 8.3

Back on track

What are my values?	What are my goals?	What obstacles might get in the way?	What exercises and practical solutions can I use to deal with obstacles?	How can I be kind to myself?
Attentiveness as a mother	Play Lego with my son every day 3-4pm; read to my son for 30 minutes each day	**Internal obstacles** _Thoughts_ 'What if I have a terrible disease this time?'	**Exercises** Mindful walking (Chapter 2) – on the way to and from work	Take time for myself, and do things that I enjoy Remind myself that I am doing my best, and that no one is perfect
Competence at work	Complete Module 2 of my programming course over the next week	I'll just have a quick look at the internet, to check that my symptoms aren't serious'	I'm having the thought that . . .' (Chapter 3) – when thoughts take control	
Taking care of myself	Spend one hour each day practising techniques from The Little Anxiety Workbook; take one hour each day to have a relaxing bath, read or watch TV	I don't deserve to look after myself – my son needs me and I have too much to do' _Feelings_ Fear Boredom Racing heart **External obstacles** My laptop needs a new battery	Beyond good and bad (Chapter 5) – when feelings stop me doing what I want to **Practical solutions** Call computer repair shop tomorrow	Read my Compassionate Letter when my mind is criticising me Hand on heart (Chapter 6) – when my mind is criticising me

The last word

This is the end of the chapter, so congratulations once again. You are now fully prepared for the next steps on your journey. Those steps might simply be continuing to apply the ideas and techniques presented in this book. Or you might wish to explore Acceptance and Commitment Therapy further by consulting other books, apps or online resources (see the *Recommended reading* and *Further resources* sections). Or, better still, you might want to seek out face-to-face therapy – remember that no book can substitute for an appropriately trained therapist. But however you choose to proceed, please keep on making use of whichever techniques from this book have been helpful to you.

Please remember to be kind to yourself – it is natural to feel anxious, and we all struggle in one way or another. And please remember that you have the courage and resilience to reclaim your life from anxiety, and the skills and resources that you need. You have already started and need only to keep on going, towards living the life you want, and being the person you want to be. We wish you well on this journey.

Michael, Elena and Michael

Recommended reading

Forsyth, J.P. & Eifert, G.H., *The Mindfulness and Acceptance Workbook for Anxiety*. New Harbinger (2016).

Goodman, E., *Your Anxiety Beast and You: A Compassionate Guide to Living in an Increasingly Anxious World*. Exisle (2020).

Harris, R., *The Happiness Trap*. Constable & Robinson (2007).

Hayes, S.C., & Smith, S., *Get Out of Your Mind and Into Your Life: The New Acceptance and Commitment Therapy*. New Harbinger (2005).

Hayes, S.C., *A Liberated Mind: The Essential Guide to ACT*. Vermillion (2019).

Kabat-Zinn, J., *Wherever You Go, There You Are: Mindfulness Meditation for Everyday Life.* Piatkus (2019).

LeJeune, C., *The Worry Trap: How to Free Yourself from Worry and Anxiety Using Acceptance and Commitment Therapy.* New Harbinger (2007).

Leonard-Curtin, A. & Leonard-Curtin, T., *The Power of Small: How to Make Tiny but Powerful Changes When Everything Feels Too Much.* Hachette (2018).

Meadows, G., *The Sleep Book: How to Sleep Well Every Night.* Orion (2014).

Neff, K. & Germer, C., *The Mindful Self-Compassion Workbook: A Proven Way to Accept Yourself, Build Inner Strength, and Thrive.* Guilford (2018).

Oliver, J. & Bennett, R., *The Mindfulness and Acceptance Workbook for Self-Esteem: Using Acceptance and Commitment Therapy to Move Beyond Negative Self-Talk and Embrace Self-Compassion.* New Harbinger (2020).

Silberstein-Tirch, L., *How to Be Nice to Yourself: The Everyday Guide to Self-Compassion: Effective Strategies to Increase Self-Love and Acceptance.* Althea (2019).

Sinclair, M. & Beadman, M., *The Little ACT Workbook: An Introduction to Acceptance and Commitment Therapy.* Crimson (2016).

Sinclair, M., Seydel, J. & Shaw, E., *Mindfulness for Busy People: Turning from Frantic and Frazzled into Calm and Composed.* (2nd Ed.) Pearson (2017).

Stoddard, J. A., *Be Mighty: A Woman's Guide to Liberation from Anxiety, Worry, and Stress Using Mindfulness and Acceptance.* New Harbinger (2020).

Tirch, D., *The Compassionate Mind Approach to Overcoming Anxiety: Using Compassion-focused Therapy.* Robinson (2012).

Wilson, K. & DuFrene, T., *Things Might Go Terribly, Horribly Wrong: A Guide to Life Liberated from Anxiety.* New Harbinger (2010).

Zurita Ona, P., *Living Beyond OCD Using Acceptance and Commitment Therapy: A Workbook for Adults.* Routledge (2021).

Further resources

Apps (for guided mindfulness practice):

- The ACT Companion: The Happiness Trap App
  www.actcompanion.com
- Headspace
  www.headspace.com
- Buddhify
  www.buddhify.com
- Insight timer
  www.insighttimer.com
- Calm
  www.calm.com

Websites (for resources, workshops, courses and more):

- Association of Contextual Behavioural Science (ACBS)
  www.contextualscience.org

- Breathworks
  www.breathworks-mindfulness.org.uk
- The Happiness Trap
  www.thehappinesstrap.com
- ACT Mindfully
  www.actmindfully.com
- The Compassionate Mind Foundation
  www.compassionatemind.co.uk
- Mindful Self-Compassion UK
  www.mindfulselfcompassionuk.com
- Self-Compassion
  www.self-compassion.org
- The Free Mindfulness Project
  www.freemindfulness.org
- Centre for Mindfulness Research and Practice
  www.bangor.ac.uk/mindfulness
- Oxford Mindfulness Centre
  www.oxfordmindfulness.org
- Palouse Mindfulness – free online course
  www.palousemindfulness.com

References

Bandelow, B. & Michaelis, S., 'Epidemiology of anxiety disorders in the 21st century.' *Dialogues in Clinical Neuroscience*, 17(3), 327–335 (2015).

Sinclair, M. & Beadman, M., *The Little ACT Workbook: An Introduction to Acceptance and Commitment Therapy: A Mindfulness-Based Guide to Living a Full and Meaningful Life*. Crimson (2016).

Hayes, S.C., Strosahl, K. D. & Wilson, K.G., *Acceptance and Commitment Therapy: An Experiential Approach to Behavior Change*. Guilford (1999).

Harris, R., *The Happiness Trap: Stop Struggling, Start Living*. Robinson (2008).

Harris, R., *The Single Most Powerful Technique for Extreme Fusion*. ACT Mindfully. https://www.actmindfully.com.au/upimages/The_Single_Most_Powerful_Technique_for_Extreme_Fusion_-_Russ_Harris_-_October_2016.pdf (2016).

van den Brink, E. & Koster, F., *Mindfulness Based Compassionate Living: A New Training Program to Deepen Mindfulness with Heartfulness.* Routledge (2015). Neff, K., *Supportive Touch.* Self-Compassion. https://self-compassion.org/exercise-4-supportive-touch/ (2020).

Harris, R., *ACT Made Simple: An Easy-to-Read Primer on Acceptance and Commitment Therapy.* (2nd Ed.) New Harbinger (2019).

Wilson, K.G., Sandoz, E.K., Kitchens, J. & Roberts, M., 'The valued living questionnaire: Defining and measuring valued action within a behavioral framework.' *The Psychological Record*, 60, 249–272 (2010).

Polk, K.L., Schoendorff, B., Webster, M. & Olaz, F.O., *The Essential Guide to the ACT Matrix: A Step-by-Step Approach to Using the ACT Matrix Model in Clinical Practice.* New Harbinger (2016).